TEST PREP READING BOOK FOR CASAS READING STEPS LEVEL D—FORMS 627R & 628R

Turning Learners into Proficient Readers while Preparing them for CASAS Reading STEPS Level D—Forms 627R & 628R

By

COACHING FOR BETTER LEARNING

TABLE OF CONTENTS

PREFACE

Dear Instructors,

Get ready to transform your ESL classroom with our *Test Prep Reading Book for CASAS Reading STEPS Level D,* specifically designed for the Form 627R & 628R reading comprehension tests. This essential tool aligns with the English Language Proficiency Standards (ELPS) for Adult Education. It satisfies the National Reporting System (NRS) and Workforce Innovation and Opportunity Act (WIOA) expectations, ensuring your ESL students are on the path to success.

This reading textbook is more than just a teaching aid; it is a comprehensive program tailored to bolster reading comprehension among ESL learners. With a structured layout of five units and one practice test, totaling 18 learner-centered reading lessons, your students will navigate essential topics like basic communication, consumer economics, community resources, health, employment, government, and law.

Leverage Bloom's Taxonomy's six levels of objectives and competencies (remembering, understanding, applying, analyzing, evaluating, and creating) to enhance your teaching methods. Each lesson in the book is a stepping stone that equips you with the strategies to teach reading effectively, focusing on important skills such as identifying main ideas, uncovering details, making inferences, summarizing content, applying knowledge, understanding the author's perspective, and contextual vocabulary. The clarity and depth of the lessons will enable you to deliver content that resonates with your students and solidifies their understanding.

Finally, this textbook isn't just about reading—it's about providing your students with the academic and life skills they need to thrive. As they progress through the book, they'll gain valuable insights and abilities to navigate the complexities of community life, family responsibilities, and the workplace. By using this book, you'll be equipping your students for standardized testing and real-world challenges.

INTRODUCTION

Dear Students,

This book is your guide to preparing for the CASAS Reading STEPS level D test. It's filled with lessons to help you read better.

The book has five units and one practice test. Each unit has two to five lessons, for a total of 18 lessons. The lessons teach important skills like basic communication, understanding money, finding community help, staying healthy, finding a job, and learning about government and laws. These skills will help you in many parts of your life.

When you read this book, you will interact with different texts and information about reading and real-world activities. After you read, you will answer questions. These questions make sure you understand the main points, details, the writer's thoughts, and the words they use.

Remember, reading is a skill that gets better as you use it. This book is a unique tool. It will teach you about school and life and give you information to help you in your community, with your family, and at work.

Good luck as you practice your reading! Every lesson you finish will take you closer to your goals.

Reading Strategies:

Here are ten ways you can improve your reading comprehension skills:

1. Preview the text: Look at titles and subtitles to get an idea of what you will read.

2. Set a purpose: Decide why you are reading. Is it to answer a question or learn something new?

3. Read aloud daily: This can help you better understand texts. The more you read, the better you will get.

4. Use pictures: They can help you guess and understand the text.

5. Re-read: If you don't understand something, read it again.

6. Summarize: After reading, tell yourself what the text was about.

7. Ask questions: While reading, ask, "Who, what, where, when, why, and how?"

8. Make connections: Relate the text to your own life or things you already know.

9. Learn to infer: Guess what the author means based on clues in the text.

10. Use a dictionary: If you don't know a word, look it up.

Vocabulary Building:

Here are seven strategies to increase your vocabulary:

Strategy	Description
Find synonyms.	Look for words that mean the same as new words you find.
Use the words.	Try to use new words in sentences of your own.
Make flashcards.	Write new words on cards with their meanings.
Create a vocabulary journal.	Keep a notebook of new words and their meanings.
Read regularly.	The more you read, the more words you will learn.
Learn word parts.	Study prefixes, suffixes, and roots to understand more words.
Play word games.	Games like crosswords can help you learn new words.

Keep going; you can do it!

Lesson 1: Goods and Services

Objectives

1. Students will read short texts and answer questions about goods and services.

2. Students will analyze descriptive texts to interpret information, identify main ideas, and understand perspectives related to purchasing decisions.

Exercise 1- Draw a line connecting each word to its correct definition.

Word	Meaning
Invoice	A detailed list of sold goods
Warranty	The action of buying or selling goods or services
Retailer	A reduction in price
Consumer	A marketing effort to increase sales
Promotion	A person who buys products
Discount	A business that sells goods
Refund	A promise about the quality of a product
Transaction	Money returned to a customer

Exercise 2- Read the text below before answering the questions.

Smart Consumer Choices in Electronics

Linda is in the market for a new computer. Her old one has become slow and cannot keep up with the latest software updates. After researching several brands and models, she decides to focus on those offering the best balance between performance and price. Linda first reads online reviews and watches tutorial videos to see the computers in action. Secondly, she visits local electronics stores to test the models she likes. She speaks with the sales representatives to get more information about warranty terms and support services. This firsthand experience helps her narrow down her choices. She then waits for a seasonal sale event, making use of a special promotion that includes an extended warranty. Her final choice is a high-performance computer that meets all her requirements. She purchases it online to take advantage of an additional online-only discount. The store confirms her purchase with an emailed invoice, which Linda saves for her records.

Comprehension Questions:

1. What factors are influencing Linda's computer purchase?

____

2. How does Linda use reviews and videos in her decision-making process?

____

3. What benefits does Linda find in speaking directly with sales representatives?

____

4. Explain the timing of Linda's purchase. Why does she wait for a sale?

____

5. What steps does Linda take to ensure her purchase is documented?

____

Exercise 3- Read the text below before answering the questions.

Buying a Car

Michael needs a new car as his current vehicle is no longer reliable. He starts by setting a budget and listing the features that are most important to him, such as fuel efficiency and safety ratings. He uses various car comparison websites to find several models that fit his criteria. Next, Michael visits car dealerships to see the cars in person and test drives a few selected models. During these visits, he pays close attention to the cars' handling and comfort. He also discusses financing options and trade-in values for his old car, ensuring he understands all the financial implications. After considering all factors, Michael selects a car that offers the best combination of features and price. He negotiates the final price with the dealer, including some additional benefits like free maintenance for a year. Michael finalizes the purchase and receives a detailed contract outlining every aspect of the deal, giving him confidence in his decision.

Comprehension Questions:

1. What initial steps does Michael take to start his car purchase?

____

2. How does personal experience influence his car choice?

____

3. Discuss the importance of financial discussions in Michael's decision-making process.

____

4. What factors contribute to Michael's final decision on which car to buy?

____

5. How does Michael ensure his understanding and satisfaction with the purchase?

____

Exercise 4- Read the advertisement below before answering the questions.

Sales Advertisement: SUV Winter Sale

Features	Details
Model	2024 Adventure SUV
Price Cut	$3,000 off
Special Offer	Free winter tires and maintenance
Available Until	Until stocks last
Financing	0% APR for the first year

Comprehension Questions:

1. What model and discount are offered in this SUV sale?

____

2. What special offer comes with the SUV purchase?

____

3. What does "Available Until" indicate about the sale?

____

4. How does the financing option add value for buyers?

____

5. How might the special offers influence a potential buyer's decision?

____

Exercise 5- Fill in the blanks with the correct words (*promotion, retailers, warranty, refund, invoice*).

1. The customer was happy to receive a full _________ for the defective product.

2. Shopping during a _________ can save you a lot of money.

3. Make sure to read the _________ carefully to ensure all the items you ordered are listed.

4. Always ask about the _________ when buying expensive items.

5. Compare prices and features at different _________ to get the best deal.

Exercise 6- Dictation

Your teacher will read some of the new words from Exercise 1. Write down what you hear.

____

____

Exercise 7- Writing

Write a paragraph to summarize what you know and learned about shopping for cars or electronics.

____

____

____

____

____

ANSWER KEYS

Exercise 1- Vocabulary Matching:
1. Invoice - A detailed list of sold goods
2. Warranty - A promise about the quality of a product
3. Retailer - A business that sells goods
4. Consumer - A person who buys products
5. Promotion – A marketing effort to increase sales
6. Discount - A reduction in price
7. Refund - Money returned to a customer
8. Transaction - Action of buying or selling

Exercise 2- Text 1:
1. Factors influencing Linda's purchase include performance, price, reviews, warranty terms, and seasonal sales.
2. Linda uses reviews and videos to visually assess the computers and gather user feedback.
3. Speaking with sales representatives helps Linda learn about warranties and support services that influence her decision.
4. Linda waits for a sale to take advantage of additional benefits, such as an extended warranty, to get the best price for the computer.
5. Linda takes steps to ensure her purchase is documented by saving the emailed invoice the store sends her after confirming her purchase.

Exercise 3- Text 2:
1. Michael starts by setting a budget and listing important features. He then uses car comparison websites to identify potential models.
2. Personal test drives help him assess the cars' handling and comfort, which influences his choice.
3. Financial discussions are crucial for understanding the full cost implications, including financing and trade-in values.
4. Michael selects a car based on the features, price, handling, comfort, and additional benefits like free maintenance.
5. Michael ensures understanding and satisfaction by thoroughly reviewing the contract detailing all aspects of the deal.

Exercise 4- Sales Advertisement:
1. The model offered is the "2024 Adventure SUV" with a $3,000 discount.
2. The special offer includes free winter tires and maintenance.
3. "Available until stocks last" indicates that the offer is only available while the current stock lasts.
4. The 0% APR financing for the first year adds financial value by reducing the cost of borrowing.
5. The special offers, like price cuts and free additions, make the SUV purchase more appealing and cost-effective.

Exercise 5- Fill-in-the-Blanks:
1. refund
2. promotion
3. invoice
4. warranty
5. retailers

Lesson 2: Housing and Services

Objectives:

1. Students will learn key vocabulary related to housing and housing services.

2. Students will read and answer questions on comparing housing options and the procedures involved in securing housing.

Exercise 1- Draw a line connecting each word to its correct definition.

Word	Meaning
Realtor	A person who has the legal right to live on a property
Foreclosure	A person who helps you buy or sell a house
Lease	Payment made regularly for housing
Mortgage	The process of losing property due to unpaid mortgage
Tenant	A contract to rent a property
Down Payment	Money paid at the start of buying a house
Equity	The value of a property minus the debt
Subsidy	Financial help from the government

Exercise 2- Read the text below before answering the questions.

Finding the Right Home

Finding the right home involves several steps. First, you need to determine your budget. Understanding what you can afford helps in narrowing down your choices. You may consider the location, the size of the house, and the type of neighborhood. Some people prioritize being close to work, while others look for good schools and parks. After deciding on your preferences, you can start searching for houses. Many people use online platforms or hire a realtor to help with the process. Realtors can provide valuable insights and show houses that match your criteria.

When you find a potential home, it's essential to inspect it thoroughly. Look at the condition of the house and consider any repairs that may be needed. The next step is making an offer. If the offer is accepted, you will need to secure a mortgage. A down payment is typically required, which is a percentage of the total price. After the financial arrangements are complete, the final step is closing the deal. This involves signing the lease or purchase agreement and paying the necessary fees. Congratulations, you now own a home!

Comprehension Questions:

1. What should you determine first when looking for a home?

____

2. Why might someone prioritize being close to work when choosing a home?

____

3. What is the role of a realtor in the home-buying process?

____

4. Why is it important to inspect a potential home thoroughly?

____

5. What does the final step involve in securing a home?

____

6. Summarize each paragraph in your own words.

____

Exercise 3- Read the text below before answering the questions.

Navigating the Housing Market

The housing market can be competitive and challenging. Prices fluctuate based on demand and supply. In a seller's market, there are more buyers than available houses, often leading to bidding wars. In contrast, a buyer's market offers more choices and often better deals for buyers. It's essential to understand the current market conditions before making any decisions. Keeping an eye on market trends and prices can give you an edge. Some people wait for the market to cool down to get a better deal, while others act quickly to secure a home.

Once you've decided to enter the housing market, you should prepare all necessary documents. This includes proof of income, credit reports, and identification. A good credit score is crucial as it affects your mortgage rates. It's also advisable to get pre-approved for a mortgage. Pre-approval shows sellers that you are serious and capable of purchasing the house. During this process, you may also encounter terms like 'equity' and 'subsidy.' Understanding these terms is important for making informed decisions. Always read the fine print in any agreement before signing.

Comprehension Questions:

1. What is a seller's market?

____

2. Why is it important to understand market conditions before buying a home?

____

3. What documents should you prepare when entering the housing market?

____

4. How does a good credit score affect your mortgage rates?

____

5. Why is it important to get pre-approved for a mortgage?

____

6. Summarize each paragraph in your own words.

____

Exercise 4- Read the advertisement below before answering the questions.

Houses	Details
House A	$300,000, near good schools, 5 parks, walk score: 80
House B	$320,000, local grant available, near downtown, 3 parks

Comprehension Questions:

1. What is the price difference between House A and House B?

____

2. Which house is closer to downtown?

____

3. How many parks are near House A?

____

4. Which house has a local grant available?

____

5. What is the walk score of House A?

____

6. Which house is more expensive?

____

Exercise 5- Fill in the blanks with the correct words (*lease, subsidy, down payment, foreclosure, realtor*).

1. The _____________ helps you find a suitable house to buy.

2. A _____________ is required when buying a house, usually a percentage of the total price.

3. Losing your house due to unpaid debts is called _____________.

4. _____________ is the contract you sign when renting a property.

5. Financial help from the government for housing is known as a _____________.

Exercise 6- Dictation

Your teacher will read some of the new words from Exercise 1. Write down what you hear.

____

____

Exercise 7- Writing

Write a paragraph to summarize what you know and learned about buying a home.

____

____

____

____

____

____

____

____

ANSWER KEYS

Exercise 1- Vocabulary Matching:
1. Realtor - A person who helps you buy or sell a house
2. Foreclosure – The process of losing property due to unpaid mortgage
3. Lease – A contract to rent a property
4. Mortgage - Payment made regularly for housing
5. Tenant – A person who has the legal right to live on a property
6. Down Payment - Money paid at the start of buying a house
7. Equity – The value of a property minus the debt
8. Subsidy - Financial help from the government

Exercise 2- Text 1:
1. You should determine your budget.
2. Someone might prioritize this to reduce the time it takes to get to work and to make travel more convenient.
3. A realtor helps in the home-buying process by providing valuable insights and showing houses that match what you want.
4. It is important to check its condition and identify any necessary repairs.
5. The final step involves signing the lease or purchase agreement and paying any necessary fees.
6. Paragraph 1: The process of finding a home involves determining your budget, choosing a location, and considering preferences.
Paragraph 2: Once a potential home is found, it's important to inspect it, make an offer, secure financing, and finalize the purchase.

Exercise 3- Text 2:
1. A seller's market occurs when there are more buyers than houses.
2. Understanding market conditions helps you make informed decisions about when to buy and what kind of deal you can expect.
3. You should prepare proof of income, credit reports and identification.
4. A good credit score can result in lower mortgage rates
5. It shows sellers that you are financially capable of purchasing a home, giving you an advantage.
6. Paragraph 1: The differences between a seller's and a buyer's market are explained, emphasizing the importance of understanding market conditions.
Paragraph 2: Key steps when entering the housing market include preparing documents, maintaining good credit, getting pre-approved, and understanding specific terms.

Exercise 4- Sales Advertisement:
1. The price difference is $20,000.
2. House B is closer to downtown.
3. There are 5 parks.
4. House B has a local grant.
5. The walk score is 80.
6. House B is more expensive.

Exercise 5- Fill-in-the-Blanks:
1. Realtor
2. Down payment
3. Foreclosure
4. Lease
5. Subsidy

Lesson 3: Managing Household Finances

Objectives:

1. Students will learn key vocabulary related to household finances and budgeting.

2. Students will develop skills to create and manage a household budget.

Exercise 1- Draw a line connecting each word to its correct definition.

Word	Meaning
Budget	Money kept for future use
Expense	Money paid for using someone else's property
Income	Money set aside for unexpected costs
Savings	Money borrowed to buy a house, usually repaid in monthly payments
Investment	Money spent on goods and services
Mortgage	The money you earn from work or investments
Rent	A plan for income and spending
Emergency Fund	Money put into something to earn more money

Exercise 2- Read the text below before answering the questions.

Creating a Household Budget

Creating a household budget is essential for managing finances. A budget helps you plan how to use your money. Start by listing your monthly income. This includes all the money you receive, like salaries or investments. Next, list your expenses. These are things you spend money on, like rent, utilities, and groceries. It's important to separate fixed expenses from variable expenses. Fixed expenses, like rent or mortgage payments, do not change. Variable expenses, like groceries and entertainment, can change each month.

Once you have a list of your income and expenses, calculate the total for each. Subtract your total expenses from your total income to see if you have money left over. This leftover money can go into savings or investments. If your expenses are higher than your income, you need to find ways to cut costs. Look for unnecessary expenses you can reduce or eliminate. A budget helps you make better financial decisions and ensures you have money for important things, like savings and emergencies. Reviewing your budget regularly is important to keep it accurate and useful.

Comprehension Questions:

1. What is the purpose of creating a household budget?

____

2. What should you list first when creating a budget?

____

3. What is the difference between fixed and variable expenses?

____

4. What should you do if your expenses are higher than your income?

____

5. Why is it important to review your budget regularly?

____

6. Summarize each paragraph in your own words.

____

Exercise 3- Read the text below before answering the questions.

Saving for the Future

Saving money is an important part of managing household finances. It helps you prepare for future needs and emergencies. There are different ways to save money. One way is to open a savings account at a bank. A savings account is a safe place to keep your money and earn interest. Another way to save money is by setting aside a portion of your income each month. This is called automatic savings. You can set up a direct deposit from your paycheck into your savings account.

Investing is another way to grow your savings. Investments can include buying stocks, bonds, or real estate. Unlike a savings account, investing can bring higher returns but also comes with risks. It's important to understand these risks before investing your money. An emergency fund is also crucial. This is money saved for unexpected expenses, like car repairs or medical bills. Having an emergency fund helps you avoid debt and provides financial security. The key to successful saving and investing is consistency and careful planning.

Comprehension Questions:

1. Why is saving money important?

____

2. What is a savings account?

____

3. What is the benefit of automatic savings?

____

4. How is investing different from saving?

____

5. Why is having an emergency fund important?

____

6. Summarize each paragraph in your own words.

____

Exercise 4- Read the text below before answering the questions.

Managing Debt and Expenses

Managing debt is a critical part of household finances. Debt includes any money you owe, like credit card balances or loans. It's important to pay off debt as quickly as possible. High-interest debt, like credit cards, should be paid off first. This type of debt can quickly become expensive if not managed properly. One way to manage debt is by creating a repayment plan. A repayment plan outlines how much you will pay each month until the debt is gone. This helps you stay on track and avoid missed payments.

In addition to managing debt, it's important to keep track of your expenses. This means knowing where your money goes each month. You can use a notebook, a spreadsheet, or a budgeting app to track expenses. Keeping track of expenses helps you identify areas where you can save money. For example, if you spend a lot on eating out, you might cook more meals at home. Reducing unnecessary expenses can free up money for savings or paying off debt. Effective management of debt and expenses leads to better financial health and peace of mind.

Comprehension Questions:

1. What should be paid off first when managing debt?

____

2. What is the purpose of a repayment plan?

____

3. How can tracking expenses help you save money?

____

4. What tool can you use to track your expenses?

____

5. What is the benefit of reducing unnecessary expenses?

____

6. Summarize each paragraph in your own words.

____

Exercise 5- Read the household budget for the Ramirez family below before answering the questions.

Income	Amount
Salary	$3,500
Investments	$500
Total Income	$4,000
Expenses	**Amount**
Rent	$1,200
Utilities	$200
Groceries	$400
Transportation	$150
Insurance	$100
Entertainment	$100
Total Expenses	$2,150
Savings & Investments	**Amount**
Savings	$500
Vacation Fund	$150

Emergency Fund	$200
Investments	$500
Total Savings & Investments	$1,350

Comprehension Questions:

1. What is the total monthly income for the Ramirez family?

____

2. How much do they spend on rent?

____

3. What is the total amount allocated for savings and investments?

____

4. How much is spent on entertainment each month?

____

5. What could the Ramirez family do if they want to save more money?

____

Exercise 6- Fill in the blanks with the correct words: Savings account, emergency fund, income, expense, budget.

1. A ___________ helps you plan how to spend your money each month.

2. An ___________ is money saved for unexpected expenses.

3. Your monthly ___________ is all the money you earn in a month.

4. A ___________ is a type of account to keep your money safely and earn a small interest.

5. Your ___________ is money spent on goods and services.

Exercise 7- Dictation

Your teacher will read some of the new words from Exercise 1. Write down what you hear.

____

____

____

Exercise 8- Writing

Write a paragraph to summarize what you know and learned about managing household expenses.

ANSWER KEYS

Exercise 1- Vocabulary Matching:
1. Budget - A plan for income and spending
2. Expense - Money spent on goods and services
3. Income - The money you earn from work or investments
4. Savings – Money kept for future use
5. Investment - Money put into something to earn more money
6. Mortgage - Money borrowed to buy a house, usually repaid in monthly payments
7. Rent - Money paid for using someone else's property
8. Emergency Fund - Money set aside for unexpected costs

Exercise 2- Text 1:
1. The purpose of a budget is to manage your money and plan how to use it effectively.
2. You should list your monthly income first.
3. Fixed expenses do not change while variable expenses can change.
4. You should cut costs.
5. It is important to keep it accurate and useful.
6. The first paragraph explains the importance of creating a budget, starting with listing income and separating fixed expenses from variable expenses.
   The second paragraph discusses calculating total income and expenses, adjusting your budget if expenses exceed income, and reviewing the budget regularly.

Exercise 3- Text 2:
1. It helps you prepare for future needs and emergencies.
2. A savings account is a bank account where money is kept safe and earns interest.
3. The benefit of automatic savings is that a portion of your income is automatically set aside each month, making it easier to save consistently.
4. Investing can bring higher returns but also has risks, unlike savings.
5. An emergency fund covers unexpected expenses and helps you avoid going into debt.
6. The first paragraph explains the importance of saving money and introduces ways to save, such as using a savings account and setting up automatic savings.
   The second paragraph discusses investing as a way to grow savings, the importance of understanding investment risks, and the need for an emergency fund for financial security.

Exercise 4- Text 3:
1. High-interest debt, like credit card balances, should be paid off first.
2. A repayment plan outlines monthly payments and helps you stay on track and avoid missed payments.
3. Tracking expenses helps you identify where to cut costs so you can save more money.
4. You can use a notebook, spreadsheet, or budgeting app.
5. Reducing unnecessary expenses frees up money that can be used for savings or paying off debt.
6. The first paragraph explains the importance of managing debt, prioritizing high-interest debt, and creating a repayment plan to stay on track with payments.
   The second paragraph discusses the importance of tracking expenses to identify where you can reduce unnecessary spending and save more.

Exercise 5- Household Budget for the Ramirez Family:
1. The total monthly income is $4,000.
2. They spend $1,200 on rent.
3. The amount allocated for savings and investments is $1,350.
4. They spend $100 on entertainment.
5. They could reduce their entertainment expenses or increase their savings amount.

Exercise 6- Fill-in-the-Blanks:
1. Budget
2. Emergency fund
3. Income
4. Savings account
5. Expense

Lesson 4: Consumer Protection Measures and Tips

Objectives:

1. Students will learn key vocabulary related to consumer protection and rights.

2. Students will read and answer questions on the basic principles of consumer protection measures and how to apply them in real-life situations.

Exercise 1- Draw a line connecting each word to its correct definition.

Word	Meaning
Refund	A statement expressing dissatisfaction with a product or service
Fraud	The action of removing a defective product from the market
Warranty	To give something in return for something else
Complaint	A written guarantee promising to repair or replace a product if necessary.
Recall	Small details in an agreement with important details
Consumer	To give back money for returned goods
Fine Print	A person who buys goods and services
Exchange	Deception intended for financial gain

Exercise 2- Read the text below before answering the questions.

Understanding Warranties and Refunds

A warranty is a promise from a manufacturer to fix or replace a product if it breaks within a certain time. Warranties can provide peace of mind for consumers, ensuring they are covered if something goes wrong. It's important to read the warranty details to know what is included and what is not. Sometimes, only specific parts or types of damages are covered. When purchasing a product, understanding the refund policy is equally important. Some stores allow refunds within a certain period if a product is returned in its original condition. Other stores might only offer store credit or exchanges.

However, not all refund policies are straightforward. Some require a receipt or original packaging. It's also possible that a restocking fee will be charged. Understanding these details helps consumers make informed decisions. Knowing your rights can prevent frustration and ensure a smoother shopping experience. Always keep your receipts and be aware of the return policy before buying.

Comprehension Questions

1. What is a warranty?

2. Why is it important to read the warranty details?

3. What might some stores offer instead of a refund?

4. What should consumers do with their receipts?

5. Why is understanding refund policies crucial?

6. Summarize each paragraph in your own words.

Exercise 3- Read the text below before answering the questions.

Identifying and Avoiding Fraud

Fraud is a deceptive practice intended to result in financial or personal gain. It can take many forms, from fake products to misleading advertisements. Consumers must stay vigilant to avoid falling victim to fraud. One common form of fraud is phishing, where scammers try to obtain sensitive information by pretending to be trustworthy entities. They might send emails that look official, asking for passwords or credit card numbers.

To protect yourself, always verify the source of any request for personal information. Check for secure website indicators like a padlock icon in the browser. Avoid deals that seem too good to be true, as they often are. Report any suspicious activity to the authorities to help prevent others from becoming victims. By staying informed and cautious, consumers can protect their personal and financial information.

Comprehension Questions

1. What is fraud?

____

2. What is phishing, and how does it work?

____

3. How can consumers protect themselves from phishing?

____

4. What should you do if you encounter suspicious activity?

____

5. Why is it important to report fraud?

____

6. Summarize each paragraph in your own words.

____

Exercise 4- Read the text below before answering the questions.

The Importance of Reading Fine Print

The fine print in agreements often contains crucial details that affect the overall terms. Whether you're signing up for a new credit card, renting an apartment, or buying a car, it's essential to read the fine print. This text can include information about fees, interest rates, and penalties. Ignoring these details can lead to unexpected costs and complications later on. For example, a seemingly small fee in the fine print can add up over time, significantly increasing the total cost.

In some cases, the fine print may also outline restrictions or obligations you must follow. These could include conditions for canceling a contract or requirements for maintaining a service. By understanding the fine print, you can make more informed decisions and avoid surprises. Always take the time to read and understand all parts of a contract before agreeing to it.

Comprehension Questions

1. What is often included in the fine print of agreements?

____

2. Why is it essential to read the fine print?

____

3. How can ignoring the fine print affect you?

____

4. What kind of obligations might the fine print contain?

____

5. Why should you take the time to understand all parts of a contract?

____

6. Summarize each paragraph in your own words.

____

Exercise 5- Read the poster below before answering the questions.

Consumer Protection Poster

Number	Tips and Strategies
1	Read the fine print in all contracts.
2	Keep all receipts and proof of purchase.
3	Understand your warranty terms.
4	Report fraudulent activities immediately.
5	Check for secure websites when shopping online.
6	Be cautious of deals that seem too good to be true.
7	Know your rights as a consumer.
8	Use secure payment methods.
9	Do not share personal information online without verification.
10	Read reviews and do research before buying.

Comprehension Questions

1. What should you do with all receipts and proof of purchase?

____

2. Why is it important to understand warranty terms?

____

3. What action should you take if you encounter fraudulent activities?

____

4. How can you verify if a website is secure for shopping?

____

5. Why is it important to read reviews and do research before making a purchase?

____

Exercise 6- Fill in the blanks with the correct words (*receipts, consumer, personal, fine print, payment*).

1. Always know your rights as a ___________.

2. Keep all ___________ and proof of purchase.

3. Always read the ___________ before signing a contract.

4. Use secure ___________ methods when making purchases.

5. Do not share ___________ information without verification.

Exercise 7- Dictation

Your teacher will read some of the new words from Exercise 1. Write down what you hear.

____

____

Exercise 8- Writing

Write a paragraph to summarize what you know and learned about consumer protection and rights.

____

____

____

____

____

____

ANSWER KEYS

Exercise 1- Vocabulary Matching:
1. Refund - To give back money for returned goods
2. Fraud - Deception intended for financial gain
3. Warranty - A written guarantee promising to repair or replace a product if necessary.
4. Complaint - A statement expressing dissatisfaction with a product or service
5. Recall - The action of removing a defective product from the market
6. Consumer - A person who buys goods and services
7. Fine Print - Small details in an agreement with important details
8. Exchange - To give something in return for something else

Exercise 2- Text 1:
1. A warranty is a promise from a manufacturer to fix or replace a product if it malfunctions within a certain time.
2. It is important to understand it to know what is covered and what is not in the warranty.
3. Some stores might offer store credit or exchanges.
4. Consumers should keep them so they can return or exchange items according to the store's policy.
5. Understanding refund policies helps you make informed decisions, which prevents frustration and allows you to have a smoother shopping experience.
6. Paragraph 1: Warranties are manufacturer promises to repair or replace products, so it's important to understand what's covered. Paragraph 2: Knowing refund policies and your consumer rights is essential, as policies vary by store.

Exercise 3- Text 2:
1. Fraud is a deceptive practice intended to result in financial or personal gain.
2. Phishing is a type of fraud where scammers pretend to be trustworthy entities to obtain sensitive information.
3. Consumers can verify sources and look for secure website indicators.

4. You should report suspicious activities to authorities.
5. Reporting fraud is important because it helps protect others from becoming victims.
6. Paragraph 1: Fraud is a dishonest practice for financial or personal gain, and consumers must be cautious of scams like phishing. Paragraph 2: Protect yourself by staying vigilant and reporting suspicious activity.

Exercise 4- Text 3:
1. The fine print often includes details, such as fees, interest rates, and penalties.
2. It is essential to read the fine print to understand all the important details that can affect the overall terms of the agreement.
3. Ignoring the fine print can lead to unexpected costs and complications.
4. The fine print might contain conditions for canceling contracts or requirements for maintaining services.
5. You should take the time to understand all parts of a contract to make informed decisions and avoid surprises.
6. Paragraph 1: Reading the fine print is crucial to avoid unexpected fees and complications. Paragraph 2: Understanding obligations and restrictions in the fine print helps you make informed decisions and avoid surprises.

Exercise 5- Consumer Protection Poster:
1. You should keep them as proof of purchase and for returns or warranty claims.
2. It is important so you know what is covered and what is not. Also, you would know the conditions for repairing or replacing a product if needed.
3. Report them to the authorities immediately.
4. Check for secure website indicators like a padlock icon in the browser.
5. Reading reviews and doing research helps you make informed decisions and avoid buying poor-quality products or falling for scams.

Exercise 6- Fill-in-the-Blanks:
1. Consumer
2. Receipts
3. Fine print
4. Payment
5. Personal

Lesson 5 - Using and Maintaining Personal Possessions

Objectives

1. Students will learn vocabulary related to the care, maintenance, and use of personal possessions.

2. Students will read and answer questions on procedures for maintaining cars, houses, and computers.

Exercise 1- Draw a line connecting each word to its correct definition.

Word	Meaning
Warranty	A place to keep items
Maintenance	A legal contract that grants the right to use or occupy property for a specified period
Security	Protection against financial loss due to unforeseen events
Storage	A guarantee of product quality
Insurance	Measures taken to protect against theft or damage
Service	The process of improving a system or equipment
Lease	Regular care to prevent damage
Upgrade	Professional maintenance, repair or support

Exercise 2- Read the text below before answering the questions.

Car Maintenance

Owning a car requires understanding and performing regular maintenance tasks. These tasks include checking the oil, tire pressure, and brakes to ensure the vehicle's safety and efficiency. It is recommended to change the oil every 3,000 to 5,000 miles depending on the car's make and model. Regular servicing by a professional mechanic can prevent major issues and extend the car's lifespan. Keeping the car clean both inside and out is also part of regular maintenance. Insurance is a crucial aspect of car ownership, providing financial protection in case of accidents or damage. Moreover, updating insurance policies annually ensures adequate coverage.

To maintain the car's value, owners should keep detailed records of all services and repairs. These records can help when selling the car or filing insurance claims. In addition to routine checks, drivers should be aware of any unusual sounds or changes in performance, which might indicate a problem. Prompt attention to such issues can prevent costly repairs. Lastly, it's important to follow the manufacturer's maintenance schedule and recommendations. Doing so not only ensures the vehicle's safety but also its reliability.

Comprehension Questions:

1. What are some regular maintenance tasks for cars?

____

2. How often should oil be changed?

____

3. Why is keeping service records important?

____

4. What should car owners do if they notice unusual sounds?

____

5. Why is it important to update insurance policies annually?

____

6. Summarize each paragraph in your own words.

____

Exercise 3- Read the text below before answering the questions.

House Maintenance

Maintaining a house involves various tasks to keep it safe and comfortable. These tasks include checking for leaks, cleaning gutters, and inspecting the roof for damage. Homeowners should also ensure that heating and cooling systems are serviced regularly. Changing air filters every three months can improve air quality and efficiency. Regular maintenance helps to prevent major problems and extends the life of home systems. Installing smoke detectors and testing them monthly is crucial for safety. It's also wise to have a home insurance policy that covers potential damage from natural disasters.

In addition to structural maintenance, keeping the home clean and organized is important. This includes regularly vacuuming, dusting, and cleaning appliances. Homeowners should also pay attention to outdoor areas, such as maintaining the garden and trimming trees. Proper care of the exterior, including painting and repairing fences, can enhance the home's appearance and value. Finally, homeowners should keep an emergency kit with essential items like water, food, and medical supplies in case of unexpected events.

Comprehension Questions:

1. Why is regular maintenance important?

____

2. How often should air filters be changed?

____

3. Why are smoke detectors important?

____

4. What should be included in a home insurance policy?

____

5. What is the benefit of maintaining outdoor areas?

____

6. Summarize each paragraph in your own words.

____

Exercise 4- Read the text below before answering the questions.

Computer Maintenance

Proper computer maintenance involves both software and hardware care. Regularly updating the operating system and software is crucial for security and performance. Running antivirus scans can help protect the computer from malware and other threats. It's also important to back up important data regularly, either on an external drive or through cloud storage. This ensures that data is not lost in case of a system failure. Maintaining proper storage is also key to computer health. Users should periodically clean out unnecessary files and organize their data. Defragmenting the hard drive can also improve system performance.

Physically, cleaning the keyboard and screen can prevent damage and ensure smooth operation. Additionally, ensuring adequate ventilation by keeping vents clear can prevent overheating. For laptops, taking care of the battery by avoiding overcharging can extend its life. Finally, using strong passwords and enabling two-factor authentication can protect personal information and secure the device.

Comprehension Questions:

1. What are two important software maintenance tasks for computers?

____

2. Why is backing up data important?

____

3. How can users protect their computers from viruses?

____

4. What is the purpose of defragmenting a hard drive?

____

5. How can laptop users take care of their battery?

____

6. Summarize each paragraph in your own words.

____

Exercise 5- Read the car maintenance tips below before answering the questions.

Car Maintenance Tips

1. Check oil levels regularly.

2. Inspect tire pressure monthly.

3. Replace brake pads when needed.

4. Change air filters every 15,000 miles.

5. Keep the car clean inside and out.

6. Schedule regular professional check-ups.

7. Check lights and signals.

8. Ensure proper insurance coverage.

9. Store the car in a garage if possible.

Comprehension Questions:

1. How often should tire pressure be checked?

____

2. When should air filters be changed?

____

3. Why is it important to have proper insurance coverage?

____

4. What is one benefit of storing a car in a garage?

____

Exercise 6- Read the house maintenance tips below before answering the questions.

House Maintenance Tips

1. Check for leaks regularly.
2. Clean gutters twice a year.
3. Inspect the roof annually.
4. Change air filters every three months.
5. Install smoke detectors and test them monthly.
6. Trim trees and bushes near the house.
7. Check security systems regularly.

Comprehension Questions:

1. How often should gutters be cleaned?

____

2. What should homeowners do annually regarding their roofs?

____

3. Why are smoke detectors important?

____

4. What is one reason for trimming trees and bushes near the house?

____

Exercise 7- Fill in the blanks with the correct words (*clean, backup, maintenance, oil levels, insurance*).

1. Always check the car's _____________ to avoid engine problems.

2. Homeowners should have ___________ to protect against damage.

3. It's important to ___________ computer files you do not want to lose.

4. Regular ___________ can help prevent major house repairs.

5. Keeping the car ___________ helps maintain its value.

Exercise 8- Dictation

Your teacher will read some of the new words from Exercise 1. Write down what you hear.

____

____

Exercise 9- Writing

Write a paragraph to summarize what you know and learned about maintaining and using personal possessions.

____

____

____

____

____

____

____

ANSWER KEYS

Exercise 1- Vocabulary Matching:
1. Warranty - A guarantee of product quality
2. Maintenance - Regular care to prevent damage
3. Security - Measures taken to protect against theft or damage
4. Storage - A place to keep items
5. Insurance - Protection against financial loss due to unforeseen events
6. Service - Professional maintenance, repair or support
7. Lease - A legal contract that grants the right to use or occupy property for a specified period
8. Upgrade – The process of improving a system or equipment

Exercise 2- Text 1:
1. Regular maintenance tasks for cars include checking the oil, tire pressure, and brakes.
2. Oil should be changed every 3,000 to 5,000 miles.
3. Keeping service records is important because they can help when selling the car or filing insurance claims.
4. They should address the issues promptly to avoid costly repairs.
5. It is important to ensure adequate coverage.
6. Paragraph 1: Regular car maintenance includes checking oil, tire pressure, getting mechanic services, cleaning, and updating insurance.
7. Paragraph 2: Keeping service records is important for resale and insurance. Addressing issues early and following the manufacturer's schedule ensures safety and reliability.

Exercise 3- Text 2:
1. Regular maintenance is important because it helps prevent major problems and extends the lifespan of home systems.
2. Air filters should be changed every three months.
3. Smoke detectors provide early warning of fires.
4. A home insurance policy should include coverage for potential damage from natural disasters.
5. Maintaining outdoor areas enhances the home's appearance and value.
6. Paragraph 1: Regular house maintenance, smoke detectors, and home insurance ensure safety.
7. Paragraph 2: Cleanliness, outdoor upkeep, and an emergency kit protect appearance, value, and readiness.

Exercise 4- Text 3:
1. Two software maintenance tasks are updating software and running antivirus scans.
2. Backing up data is important to prevent loss of important data if there is a system failure.
3. Users can protect their computers from viruses by using antivirus software.
4. Defragmenting the hard drive improves system performance.
5. They can take care of their battery by avoiding overcharging it.
6. Paragraph 1: Update software, run antivirus scans, back up data, and organize the hard drive for security and performance.
7. Paragraph 2: Clean the device, ensure ventilation, protect the battery, and use strong passwords for added security.

Exercise 5- Car Maintenance Tips:
1. Tire pressure should be checked monthly.
2. Air filters should be changed every 15,000 miles.
3. Proper insurance coverage protects against financial loss in case of accidents and damage.
4. Storing a car in a garage protects it from weather and potential theft.

Exercise 6- House Maintenance Tips:
1. Gutters should be cleaned twice a year.
2. They should inspect it.
3. Smoke detectors can save lives by giving an early warning of fire.
4. Trimming trees and bushes prevents damage to the house.

Exercise 7- Fill-in-the-Blanks:
1. Oil levels
2. Insurance
3. Backup
4. Maintenance
5. Clean

REFLECTION ON LEARNING

Answer the following questions and discuss your responses with your teacher or classmates.

1. What reading strategies did you learn or practice in this unit?

2. What new concepts or words did you learn?

3. What reading challenges did you face?

4. What reading strategies do you need to improve?

5. What do you want your teacher to know?

Lesson 1: Types of Transportation and Travel Information

Objectives

1. Students will learn key vocabulary related to transportation and travel information.

2. Students will read and answer questions on how to use and interpret travel-related information in the US.

Exercise 1- Draw a line connecting each word to its correct definition.

Word	Meaning
Itinerary	The cost of a ticket
Schedule	A public transportation system
Fare	A building where passengers board or disembark
Terminal	A planned route or journey
Departure	A pass for travel
Arrival	The time when a vehicle reaches its destination
Ticket	The time when a vehicle leaves
Transit	A timetable for events or activities

Exercise 2- Read the text below before answering the questions.

Using Public Transit

Public transit is an efficient way to travel in cities. Buses, trains, and subways are common forms of public transportation. They have specific schedules, and it's important to know the times and routes. Many cities provide online resources to check transit schedules and plan trips. For example, in New York City, the MTA provides an app for real-time updates. Be aware of peak and off-peak hours, which can make the journey more comfortable. Peak hours often mean crowded trains and buses. Transit apps can also provide information about any service changes or delays.

Understanding fare systems is also essential. Most public transit systems use a card or ticket that passengers swipe to pay. In some cities, you can buy tickets at kiosks or online. When using public transit, it's important to be aware of the different lines and routes. Some trains may go express and skip certain stops. It's helpful to check maps and signs for information. Knowing the location of terminals and exits is useful for planning your journey. Always have a backup plan in case of unexpected changes.

Comprehension Questions:

1. What are common forms of public transportation in cities?

____

2. How can passengers check transit schedules?

____

3. Why is it important to understand fare systems?

____

4. What can make a journey more comfortable during peak hours?

____

5. How can transit apps be helpful?

____

6. Summarize each paragraph in your own words.

____

Exercise 3- Read the text below before answering the questions.

Booking Flights

Booking a flight involves several steps. First, you need to choose your destination and dates of travel. Airlines offer various options, including direct flights and flights with layovers. It's important to check the airline's schedule and choose a convenient time. After selecting a flight, you can book tickets online, at a travel agency, or directly at the airport. When booking, you need to provide personal information and payment details. Some airlines offer special promotions or discounts for early bookings.

Before traveling, it's crucial to understand the airline's baggage policy. Some airlines charge extra for checked bags, while others include it in the ticket price. Knowing the weight limit for luggage is also important. On the day of travel, passengers should arrive at the airport early for check-in and security checks. Checking in online can save time. Boarding usually starts about 30 minutes before departure. It's important to be at the correct terminal and gate. Keeping track of departure and arrival times helps ensure a smooth journey.

Comprehension Questions:

1. What are the steps involved in booking a flight?

____

2. How can passengers book flight tickets?

____

3. Why is it important to understand an airline's baggage policy?

____

4. What should passengers do on the day of travel?

____

5. Why is it important to check departure and arrival times?

____

6. Summarize each paragraph in your own words.

____

Exercise 4- Read the text below before answering the questions.

Navigating Train Stations

Train stations can be busy places with many platforms and routes. It's important to check the schedule and know which platform your train will depart from. Many stations have digital boards displaying train times and destinations. Buying a ticket is the first step before boarding. Tickets can be purchased at ticket counters, machines, or online. Some stations have different levels for arriving and departing trains. Signs and maps can help passengers navigate the station.

Understanding the train's schedule and stops is crucial. Some trains are express and do not stop at all stations. Others may have multiple stops along the way. Knowing the final destination of the train can prevent boarding the wrong one. It's also useful to know the train's class system, such as economy or first class, as ticket prices vary. In case of delays, announcements and boards will provide updates. For long journeys, checking the availability of food services and restrooms on the train is advisable.

Comprehension Questions:

1. What should passengers check before boarding a train?

____

2. Where can passengers buy train tickets?

____

3. Why is it important to know the train's schedule and stops?

____

4. How can passengers find their way around a train station?

____

5. What information do announcements and boards provide?

____

6. Summarize each paragraph in your own words.

____

Exercise 5- Read the transportation table below before answering the questions.

Transportation Table

Transportation	Schedule	Cost
Bus	6:00 AM - 10:00 PM	$50
Train	7:00 AM - 9:00 PM	$100
Flight	8:00 AM - 8:00 PM	$300
Car Rental	24 hours	$200/day

Comprehension Questions:

1. Which transportation option is available 24 hours?

____

2. How much does a bus ticket cost?

____

3. At what time does the train service end?

____

4. What is the cost of a flight ticket?

____

Exercise 6- Read the transportation options below before answering the questions.

Transportation Options from NY to San Diego

Transportation	Departure Time	Arrival Time	Duration	Cost
Flight	6:00 AM	12:00 PM	6 hours	$300
Train	8:00 AM	8:00 PM (Next day)	36 hours	$150
Bus	7:00 AM	11:00 PM (Next day)	30 hours	$100
Car Rental	Flexible	Flexible	42 hours	$350

Comprehension Questions:

1. Which transportation option has the shortest travel time from NY to San Diego?

   a) Flight   c) Bus

   b) Train   d) Car Rental

2. How long does it take to travel by train from NY to San Diego?

   a) 6 hours   c) 30 hours

   b) 36 hours   d) 42 hours

3. What is the cost difference between traveling by bus and by car rental?

   a) $50   c) $200

   b) $150   d) $250

4. Which transportation option is the most expensive?

   a) Flight   c) Bus

   b) Train   d) Car Rental

5. If someone wants to arrive in San Diego by 12:00 PM, which transportation should they choose?

a) Flight

c) Bus

b) Train

d) Car Rental

Exercise 7- Fill in the blanks with the correct words (*fare, digital, online, check in, schedule*).

1. The ____________ board displays train times and destinations.

2. Passengers should ____________ early for their flight.

3. Knowing the ____________ system, or the payment required, helps when using public transit.

4. Booking tickets ____________ can sometimes be cheaper.

5. Always check the ____________ of your transportation.

Exercise 8- Dictation

Your teacher will read some of the new words from Exercise 1. Write down what you hear.

____

____

Exercise 9- Writing

Write a paragraph to summarize what you know and learned about the types of transportation and travel information.

____

____

____

____

____

____

____

ANSWER KEYS

Exercise 1- Vocabulary Matching:
1. Itinerary - A planned route or journey
2. Schedule - A timetable for events or activities
3. Fare - The cost of a ticket
4. Terminal - A building where passengers board or disembark
5. Departure - The time when a vehicle leaves
6. Arrival - The time when a vehicle reaches its destination
7. Ticket - A pass for travel
8. Transit – A public transportation system

Exercise 2- Text 1:
1. Common forms of transport are buses, trains, and subways.
2. They can check schedules through online resources and transit apps.
3. It is important to understand so passengers can know how and where to pay for rides.
4. Being aware of peak and off-peak hours and planning your journey accordingly can make it more comfortable.
5. Transit apps can be helpful by providing information about schedules, service changes, delays, and routes, which helps passengers plan their trips better.
6. Paragraph 1: Public transit is a convenient way to travel in cities. It's important to know the schedules and routes, which can be checked online or through transit apps, and avoid peak hours.

   Paragraph 2: Understanding how the fare system works is crucial. Knowing the different routes and being aware of terminals and exits can help with planning the journey. Always have an alternative plan in case of unexpected changes.

Exercise 3- Text 2:
1. The steps involved in booking a flight include choosing your destination and travel dates, selecting a flight option, and booking the tickets.
2. They can book tickets online, at a travel agency, or at the airport.
3. It is important to avoid extra charges and ensure your luggage meets weight limits.
4. Passengers should arrive early for check-in and security checks, and ensure they are at the correct terminal and gate for boarding.
5. Ensures smooth journey.
6. Paragraph 1: When booking a flight, you need to choose your destination, travel dates, and flight. Tickets can be booked online, at a travel agency, or at the airports. Look out for specials from some airlines.

   Paragraph 2: Understand your airline's baggage policy. On travel day, arrive early for check-in and security, and ensure you know your terminal and gate.

Exercise 4- Text 3:
1. Passengers should check the train schedule and platform number.
2. They can buy tickets at ticket counters, machines, and online.
3. Knowing the train's schedule and stops is important to avoid boarding the wrong train.
4. They can use signs and maps.
5. They provide updates on delays, train times, platforms and changes to the schedule.
6. Paragraph 1: It's important to check the train schedule and know the correct platform. Tickets can be purchased at various locations, and signs and maps can help passengers navigate the station.

   Paragraph 2: Understanding the train schedule and knowing the stops are crucial to avoid boarding the wrong train. Be aware of the train's class system and any onboard services. Announcements and boards provide updates on delays and other important information.

Exercise 5- Transportation Table:
1. The car rental is available 24 hours.
2. It costs 50 dollars.
3. The train service ends at 9:00 PM.
4. The flight ticket costs 300 dollars.

Exercise 6- Transportation Options:
1. a) Flight
2. b) 36 hours
3. d) $250
4. d) Car Rental
5. a) Flight

Exercise 7- Fill-in-the-Blanks:
1. Digital
2. Check in
3. Fare
4. Online
5. Schedule

Lesson 2: Community Agencies and Services

Objectives for the Lesson:

- Students will identify and understand key vocabulary related to community agencies and services.

- Students will demonstrate the ability to access and utilize various community resources.

Exercise 1- Draw a line connecting each word to its correct definition.

Word	Meaning
Counseling	Efforts to connect with and assist people in the community
Volunteer	A place that provides free food
Literacy Program	Directing someone to a different service or place
Shelter	Professional advice and support for personal issues
Hotline	A person who helps others without pay
Food Pantry	Phone service for immediate assistance
Referral	Education to improve basic skills
Outreach	A place for temporary housing

Exercise 2- Read the text below before answering the questions.

Accessing Counseling Services

Counseling services are vital for individuals dealing with stress, anxiety, or other personal challenges. These services are often provided by trained professionals at community centers or specialized clinics. Counseling can offer a safe and confidential environment to discuss personal issues and seek guidance. It can help individuals develop coping strategies and improve their mental health. Some counseling services are available for free or on a sliding scale, depending on the individual's income.

It's important to reach out and seek help when needed, as mental health is a crucial aspect of overall well-being. Regular sessions with a counselor can lead to significant improvements in one's life. Additionally, many communities offer group counseling sessions that provide peer support and shared experiences. Counseling services can also help individuals connect with other necessary resources, such as housing or financial aid. Utilizing these services can lead to a more balanced and healthy life.

Comprehension Questions:

1. What types of challenges are counseling services helpful for?

____

2. Where are counseling services often provided?

____

3. Why is mental health considered crucial?

____

4. What additional support can group counseling sessions provide?

____

5. How can counseling services assist beyond personal issues?

____

6. Summarize each paragraph in your own words.

____

Exercise 3- Read the text below before answering the questions.

Volunteering in the Community

Volunteering is a valuable way to give back to the community and help those in need. It involves offering your time and skills without expecting any payment in return. Volunteers can work in various settings, such as food pantries, shelters, and literacy programs. Many organizations rely on volunteers to operate and provide essential services.

This work not only benefits the community but also provides volunteers with a sense of fulfillment and purpose. It is also a great way to gain experience and enhance your resume. For individuals looking to enter a new field or build a career, volunteering can offer hands-on experience and networking opportunities. Moreover, the act of volunteering fosters a sense of community and solidarity. It can inspire others to contribute their time and efforts to worthy causes.

Comprehension Questions:

1. What is the primary benefit of volunteering for the community?

____

2. Name three places where volunteers can work.

____

3. How does volunteering benefit the volunteers themselves?

____

4. How can volunteering help with career building?

____

5. What social benefits does volunteering provide?

____

6. Summarize each paragraph in your own words.

____

Exercise 4- Read the text below before answering the questions.

Utilizing Literacy Programs

Literacy programs are designed to help individuals improve their reading and writing skills. These programs are often free and are offered at community centers, libraries, and schools. They provide essential education for adults who want to advance their careers or simply improve their ability to function in daily life. Instructors in literacy programs are usually trained to work with adult learners, understanding their unique needs and challenges.

The curriculum may include basic reading, writing, and sometimes even math skills. Participants can progress at their own pace, and the supportive environment encourages learning and growth. These programs often provide additional resources, such as access to computers and job search assistance. Completing a literacy program can open doors to further education and better job opportunities. The impact of improved literacy extends beyond the individual, benefiting their families and communities.

Comprehension Questions:

1. What are the main goals of literacy programs?

____

2. Where can people find literacy programs?

____

3. What additional resources might literacy programs offer?

____

4. How do literacy programs benefit the participants' families and communities?

____

5. Why is a supportive learning environment important in literacy programs?

____

6. Summarize each paragraph in your own words.

____

Exercise 5- Read the information below before answering the questions.

Information About 5 Community Agencies

Agency Name	Service Provided	Contact Information
Helping Hands	Food Pantry	123 Main St, (555) 123-4567
Safe Haven	Shelter	456 Elm St, (555) 987-6543
Community Care	Counseling Services	789 Oak St, (555) 246-8100
Learn & Grow	Literacy Program	321 Pine St, (555) 135-7911
Reach Out	Outreach and Referral	654 Maple St, (555) 468-1325

Comprehension Questions:

1. Which agency provides food assistance?

____

2. What type of service does Safe Haven offer?

____

3. Where is the counseling service located?

____

4. Which agency helps with literacy?

____

5.   How can people contact the outreach service?

____ 50 _______________

Exercise 6- Fill in the blanks with the correct words (*literacy, outreach, hotline, shelter, volunteer*).

1.   The _______________ program helps people improve their reading skills.

2.   If you need temporary housing, you can go to a _______________.

3.   A _______________ is someone who offers their time to help others without pay.

4.   The _______________ can provide immediate assistance through a phone call.

5.   _______________ involves efforts to connect with people in the community.

Exercise 7- Dictation

Your teacher will read some of the new words from Exercise 1. Write down what you hear.

Exercise 8- Writing

Write a paragraph to summarize what you know and learned about community agencies and services.

ANSWER KEYS

Exercise 1- Vocabulary Matching:
1. Counseling – Professional advice and support for personal issues
2. Volunteer - A person who helps others without pay
3. Literacy Program - Education to improve basic skills
4. Shelter - A place for temporary housing
5. Hotline - Phone service for immediate assistance
6. Food Pantry – A place that provides free food
7. Referral - Directing someone to a different service or place
8. Outreach - Efforts to connect with and assist people in the community

Exercise 2- Text 1:
1. Counseling services are helpful for dealing with stress, anxiety and other personal challenges.
2. They are often provided at community centers and specialized clinics.
3. Mental health is considered crucial because it is a key aspect of overall well-being.
4. Group counseling provides peer support and shared experiences.
5. Counseling services can connect individuals with other necessary resources, such as housing or financial aid.
6. Paragraph 1: Counseling services help individuals manage personal challenges and improve mental health. They can be free or adjusted based on income.
Paragraph 2: Mental health is key to overall well-being. Counseling, including group sessions, offers support and connections to other resources, leading to a healthier, more balanced life.

Exercise 3- Text 2:
1. The primary benefit is helping those in need.
2. Volunteers can work at food pantries, shelters, and literacy programs.
3. Volunteers gain a sense of fulfillment and purpose. They also learn new skills and get networking opportunities.
4. Volunteering can offer hands-on experience, enhance a resume and give networking opportunities
5. They might offer access to computers and job search assistance.

6. Volunteering fosters a sense of community and solidarity and can inspire others to contribute to worthy causes.
7. First Paragraph: Volunteering involves giving time and skills without payment to support community services. Many organizations depend on volunteers to provide essential services.
Second Paragraph: Volunteering benefits both the community and the volunteers. It can also inspire others to get involved in helping worthy causes.

Exercise 4- Text 3:
1. Literacy programs improve reading and writing skills, and sometimes math skills.
2. They can find these programs at community centers, libraries, and schools.
3. Improved literacy can provide better education and job opportunities.
4. A supportive learning environment encourages learning and growth.
5. First Paragraph: Literacy programs help individuals improve reading and writing skills for personal and professional growth, often through free programs in community centers, libraries, and schools.
Second Paragraph: The programs offer a flexible curriculum in a supportive environment, sometimes including math and additional resources like computers and job search help. Completing a program can positively impact families and communities.

Exercise 5- Information About 5 Community Agencies
1. Helping Hands offer food assistance.
2. They offer shelter.
3. The counseling service is located at 789 Oak St.
4. Learn & Grow helps with literacy.
5. People can contact them at (555) 468-1325

Exercise 6- Fill-in-the-Blanks:
1. Literacy
2. Shelter
3. Volunteer
4. Hotline
5. Outreach

Lesson 3: Understanding Aspects of Society and Culture

Objectives for the Lesson:

- Students will identify and understand key vocabulary related to society and culture in the US.

- Students will read and answer questions on cultural diversity and the importance of cultural celebrations.

Exercise 1- Draw a line connecting each word to its correct definition.

Words	Meaning
Tradition	Variety, especially of different cultures
Festival	Accepted ways of behaving in a society
Diversity	A way of doing something that is passed down from generations
Heritage	Including several cultures
Cuisine	A group of people living in the same area
Customs	A special event often with celebrations
Multicultural	Something inherited from the past
Community	A style of cooking specific to a culture

Exercise 2- Read the text below before answering the questions.

The Role of Festivals in Cultural Exchange

Festivals are an essential aspect of cultural expression. They provide a platform for communities to celebrate their heritage and traditions. In the United States, many festivals showcase the rich diversity of its population. For example, the Lunar New Year is celebrated with vibrant parades and cultural performances. Similarly, Oktoberfest brings people together to enjoy German cuisine and music. These events allow people to experience different cultures and promote understanding and acceptance.

Festivals also contribute to the economy by attracting tourists and creating jobs. They offer a space for artisans and vendors to sell traditional crafts and foods. Moreover, festivals often include educational components, such as workshops and lectures, that provide deeper insights into the culture being celebrated. Participating in these events can enrich one's knowledge of the world and foster a sense of global community. By celebrating diverse cultures, festivals help to build bridges between different communities.

Comprehension Questions:

1. What do festivals provide a platform for?

____

2. Name two festivals mentioned in the text.

____

3. How do festivals contribute to the economy?

____

4. What educational components can be found at festivals?

____

5. Why are festivals important for cultural exchange?

____

6. Summarize each paragraph in your own words.

____

Exercise 3- Read the text below before answering the questions.

The Influence of Multiculturalism in the US

The United States is known for its multicultural society. This diversity is reflected in various aspects of everyday life, including food, language, and customs. For instance, American cuisine includes influences from Italian, Chinese, Mexican, and many other culinary traditions. In many cities, it's common to hear multiple languages spoken and see celebrations of different cultural holidays. This multicultural environment enriches the social fabric of the country.

However, living in a multicultural society also presents challenges. There can be misunderstandings and conflicts due to different cultural norms and values. It is crucial for individuals to be open-minded and respectful of others' backgrounds. Schools and workplaces often have programs to promote cultural awareness and sensitivity. These efforts help to create an inclusive environment where everyone feels valued. By embracing multiculturalism, the US continues to grow as a diverse and vibrant nation.

Comprehension Questions:

1. How is multiculturalism reflected in American society?

____

2. What are some influences mentioned in American cuisine?

____

3. What challenges can arise in a multicultural society?

____

4. How do schools and workplaces promote cultural awareness?

____

5. What is the importance of embracing multiculturalism?

____

6. Summarize each paragraph in your own words.

____

Exercise 4- Read the text below before answering the questions.

The Importance of Preserving Heritage

Heritage encompasses the traditions, customs, and artifacts passed down through generations. Preserving heritage is crucial for maintaining a connection to the past and understanding one's roots. In the US, numerous cultural organizations work to preserve the heritage of various communities. Museums, historical sites, and cultural centers play a significant role in this effort. They provide spaces for people to learn about and celebrate their cultural backgrounds.

Furthermore, heritage preservation includes the conservation of traditional arts and crafts. Many communities hold workshops to teach younger generations about traditional techniques and practices. These activities not only keep traditions alive but also provide a sense of identity and pride. In a rapidly changing world, heritage offers a stable foundation and a sense of continuity. It is a reminder of where we come from and a guide for where we are going.

Comprehension Questions:

1. What does heritage include?

____

2. How do museums and cultural centers contribute to heritage preservation?

____

3. What is the role of workshops in heritage preservation?

____

4. Why is preserving heritage important?

____

5. What does heritage provide in a changing world?

____

6. Summarize each paragraph in your own words.

____

Exercise 5- Read the calendar below before answering the questions.

Calendar of International Festivals

Festival Name	Date	Location	Highlight
Diwali Festival	November 4	New York City	Fireworks, traditional dance
Chinese New Year	February 1	San Francisco	Dragon parade, lanterns
Cinco de Mayo	May 5	Los Angeles	Mexican food, mariachi music
St. Patrick's Day	March 17	Boston	Green parade, Irish dancing
Kwanzaa Celebration	December 26	Chicago	African music, storytelling

Comprehension Questions:

1. Which festival includes a dragon parade?

____

2. When is the Kwanzaa Celebration held?

____

3. What are the highlights of the St. Patrick's Day festival?

____

4. Which city hosts the Diwali Festival?

____

5. What kind of music is featured at the Cinco de Mayo festival?

____

Exercise 6- Fill in the blanks with the correct words (multicultural, diversity, St. Patrick's Day, heritage, Diwali Festival).

1. The festival celebrated in March with Irish dancing is _______________.

2. The _______________ is a celebration that includes fireworks and traditional dance.

3. Museums help in the preservation of _______________.

4. The United States is known for its _______________ society.

5. _______________ is the variety of different cultures within a society.

Exercise 7- Dictation

Your teacher will read some of the new words from Exercise 1. Write down what you hear.

____

____

Exercise 8- Writing

Write a paragraph to summarize what you know and learned about society and culture in the US.

____

____

____

____

____

____

____

ANSWER KEYS

Exercise 1- Vocabulary Matching:
1. Tradition - A way of doing something that is passed down from generations
2. Festival - A special event often with celebrations
3. Diversity - Variety, especially of different cultures
4. Heritage - Something inherited from the past
5. Cuisine - A style of cooking specific to a culture or region
6. Customs - Accepted ways of behaving in a society
7. Multicultural - Including several cultures
8. Community - A group of people living in the same area

Exercise 2- Text 1:
1. Festivals provide a platform for communities to celebrate their heritage and traditions.
2. Lunar New Year and Oktoberfest are two festivals.
3. They attract tourists and create jobs.
4. Workshops and lectures can be found at festivals.
5. Festivals allow people to experience different cultures and promote understanding and acceptance.
6. First Paragraph: Festivals offer communities a chance to celebrate their heritage. In the U.S., festivals allow people to experience various cultures, fostering understanding and acceptance.
Second Paragraph: Festivals boost the economy by attracting tourists and creating jobs. They also often include educational activities that deepen cultural knowledge.

Exercise 3- Text 2:
1. Multiculturalism is reflected in food, language, and customs.
2. It includes influences from Italian, Chinese, and Mexican culinary traditions
3. Challenges can include misunderstandings and conflicts.
4. They offer programs to promote cultural awareness and sensitivity.
5. It is important to help the US become a diverse and vibrant nation.

6. First Paragraph: The multicultural nature of the US is evident in everyday life, with diverse food, languages, and customs.
7. Second Paragraph: Multiculturalism can lead to misunderstandings, so it is important to be open-minded and respectful. Programs in schools and workplaces promote cultural awareness, helping to create an inclusive society.

Exercise 4- Text 3:
1. Heritage includes traditions, customs and artifacts.
2. They provide spaces for learning and celebrating cultural backgrounds.
3. Workshops teach younger generations traditional techniques and practices, which keep these traditions alive.
4. Preserving heritage maintains a connection to the past and provides a sense of identity.
5. Heritage provides a stable foundation and sense of continuity.
6. First Paragraph: Heritage consists of traditions, customs, and artifacts that connect people to their past. Cultural organizations, museums, and cultural centers in the US help preserve this heritage by offering spaces for learning and celebration.
Second Paragraph: Heritage preservation also involves conserving traditional arts and crafts through workshops that teach younger generations. This helps keep traditions alive, provides identity and pride, and offers stability in a rapidly changing world.

Exercise 5- Calendar of International Festivals:
1. The Chinese New Year includes a dragon parade.
2. The celebration is held on December 26.
3. The green parade and Irish dancing are the highlights.
4. New York City hosts the Diwali festival.
5. Mariachi music is featured at the festival.

Exercise 6- Fill-in-the-Blanks:
1. St. Patrick's Day
2. Diwali Festival
3. Heritage
4. Multicultural
5. Diversity

Lesson 4: Educational Systems and Services

Objectives for the Lesson:

- Students will learn key vocabulary related to the US educational system and services.

- Students will read and answer questions on the structure and services of the US educational system.

Exercise 1- Draw a line connecting each word to its correct definition.

Word	Meaning
Curriculum	The teaching staff at a school or college
Enrollment	A set of courses and their content
Tuition	An official record of a student's academic performance
Extracurricular	An official responsible for keeping student records
Faculty	The fee for instruction at a school or college
Financial Aid	Activities outside of the regular academic curriculum
Registrar	Money provided to students to help pay for education
Transcript	The process of signing up for a course or school

Exercise 2- Read the text below before answering the questions.

Navigating the US School System

The US school system consists of several levels, including pre-kindergarten (pre-K), elementary school, middle school, high school, and post-secondary education. Each level serves a specific age group and educational purpose. For example, pre-K is designed for children aged 4-5, focusing on basic skills and social development. Elementary school typically includes grades 1-5, where students learn fundamental subjects like math, reading, and science.

Middle school covers grades 6-8 and introduces more specialized subjects. High school, which includes grades 9-12, offers a broader range of courses, including elective classes. Students also have the opportunity to participate in extracurricular activities, such as sports and clubs. After high school, students may choose to attend community college, vocational school, or a four-year university. Understanding the structure of the school system helps parents and students make informed decisions about their education.

Comprehension Questions:

1. What is the purpose of pre-kindergarten in the US school system?

____

2. What grades are typically included in elementary school?

____

3. Name two types of extracurricular activities mentioned.

____

4. What options do students have after high school?

____

5. Why is it important to understand the structure of the school system?

____

6. Summarize each paragraph in your own words.

____

Exercise 3- Read the text below before answering the questions.

Understanding Financial Aid and Tuition

Paying for education can be challenging, but various financial aid options are available to help students and their families. Financial aid can come in the form of scholarships, grants, work-study programs, and loans. Scholarships and grants do not need to be repaid and are often awarded based on academic achievement or financial need. Work-study programs provide students with part-time jobs to help cover expenses.

Tuition fees vary depending on the type of institution. Community colleges usually have lower tuition costs compared to four-year universities. In addition to tuition, students may also need to pay for books, supplies, and other fees. It's important for students to complete the Free Application for Federal Student Aid (FAFSA) to determine their eligibility for federal financial aid. Proper planning and understanding of financial aid can ease the burden of educational expenses.

Comprehension Questions:

1. What are two types of financial aid that do not need to be repaid?

____

2. How do work-study programs help students?

____

3. What factors can affect the cost of tuition?

____

4. What is the purpose of completing the FAFSA?

____

5. Why is it important to understand financial aid options?

____

6. Summarize each paragraph in your own words.

____

Exercise 4- Read the text below before answering the questions.

The Role of Faculty and Curriculum in Education

Faculty members, including teachers and professors, play a crucial role in shaping students' educational experiences. They are responsible for delivering the curriculum, which consists of the courses and content that students are expected to learn. The curriculum is often designed to meet state or national education standards, ensuring that students acquire the necessary skills and knowledge.

In addition to teaching, faculty members often serve as advisors and mentors, helping students navigate academic challenges and plan their educational paths. The curriculum may include core subjects, such as math and language arts, as well as elective courses that allow students to explore their interests. By providing a well-rounded education, faculty and curriculum help prepare students for future academic and career success.

Comprehension Questions:

1. What is the role of faculty members in education?

____

2. What does the curriculum consist of?

____

3. How do elective courses benefit students?

____

4. What are two core subjects commonly included in the curriculum?

____

5. How do faculty members assist students beyond teaching?

____

6. Summarize each paragraph in your own words.

____

Exercise 5- Read the table below before answering the questions.

Table with Registration Information

Level	Age Group	Requirements	Fees	Special Services
Pre-K	4-5 years	Birth certificate, immunization	Varies	Special education, free meals
Elementary School	6-11 years	Proof of residency, registration form	Free	ESL programs, after-school care
Middle School	12-14 years	Previous school records	Free	Tutoring, extracurricular activities
High School	15-18 years	Transcript, physical exam	Free	Advanced placement courses, college counseling
Community College	18+ years	High school diploma or equivalent	Tuition varies	Financial aid, career services

Comprehension Questions:

1. What document is required for Pre-K registration?

____

2. Are there any fees for elementary school?

____

3. What services are offered to ESL students in elementary school?

____

4. What additional courses are available in high school?

____

5. What can students access through community college career services?

____

Exercise 6- Fill in the blanks with the correct words (*community college, loans, FAFSA, curriculum, faculty*).

1. The _______________ includes the courses and content taught in school.

2. Financial aid options include scholarships, grants, and _______________.

3. After high school, students may attend a _______________ or a university.

4. Teachers and professors are part of the _______________.

5. The _______________ helps determine eligibility for federal financial aid.

Exercise 7- Dictation

Your teacher will read some of the new words from Exercise 1. Write down what you hear.

____

____

Exercise 8- Writing

Write a paragraph to summarize what you know and learned about educational systems and services.

____

____

____

____

____

____

ANSWER KEYS

Exercise 1- Vocabulary Matching:
1. Curriculum - A set of courses and their content
2. Enrollment - The process of signing up for a course or school
3. Tuition - The fee for instruction at a school or college
4. Extracurricular - Activities outside of the regular academic curriculum
5. Faculty - The teaching staff at a school or college
6. Financial Aid - Money provided to students to help pay for education
7. Registrar - An official responsible for keeping student records
8. Transcript - An official record of a student's academic performance

Exercise 2- Text 1:
1. Pre-K focuses on basic skills and social development for children aged 4-5.
2. Grades 1-5 are typically included.
3. Two types of extracurricular activities are sports and clubs.
4. Students may choose to attend community college, vocational school, or a four-year university.
5. This helps parents and students make informed decisions about their education.
6. Paragraph 1: The U.S. school system includes Pre-K, Elementary (grades 1-5), Middle (grades 6-8), and High School (grades 9-12), each with specific goals.
   Paragraph 2: Middle School adds specialized subjects, and High School offers diverse courses. Afterward, students can choose Community College, Vocational School, or a Four-Year University for further education.

Exercise 3- Text 2:
1. Two types of financial aid are scholarships and grants.
2. These programs provide students with part-time jobs to cover expenses.
3. The type of institution can affect the cost.
4. The FAFSA determines eligibility for federal financial aid.

5. It is important to understand to ease the burden of educational expenses.
6. First Paragraph: Financial aid includes scholarships and grants that don't need to be repaid and work-study programs that provide part-time jobs.
   Second Paragraph: Tuition costs vary by institution, with community colleges being cheaper than four-year universities. Additional costs include books and fees. Completing the FAFSA helps determine eligibility for federal aid.

Exercise 4- Text 3:
1. Faculty members teach and mentor students.
2. The curriculum consists of courses and content students learn.
3. Elective courses allow students to explore their interests.
4. Two core subjects are math and language arts.
5. Faculty members assist students with navigating academic challenges and planning their educational paths.
6. Paragraph 1: Faculty members teach the curriculum, ensuring it meets education standards and helps students develop key skills.
   Paragraph 2: They also mentor students, guiding them through core subjects and electives for academic and career success.

Exercise 5- Table with Registration Information
1. Birth certificate and immunization are required.
2. No, elementary school is free.
3. ESL programs are offered.
4. Advanced placement courses are available.
5. Students can access financial aid and career services.

Exercise 6- Fill-in-the-Blanks:
1. Curriculum
2. Loans
3. Community college
4. Faculty
5. FAFSA

REFLECTION ON LEARNING

Answer the following questions and discuss your responses with your teacher or classmates.

1. What reading strategies did you learn or practice in this unit?

2. What new concepts or words did you learn?

3. What reading challenges did you face?

4. What reading strategies do you need to improve?

5. What do you want your teacher to know?

Lesson 1: The Health Care System and Services

Objectives for the Lesson:

- Students will learn and use key vocabulary related to healthcare access and use.

- Students will read and answer questions on the structure and services of the US healthcare system.

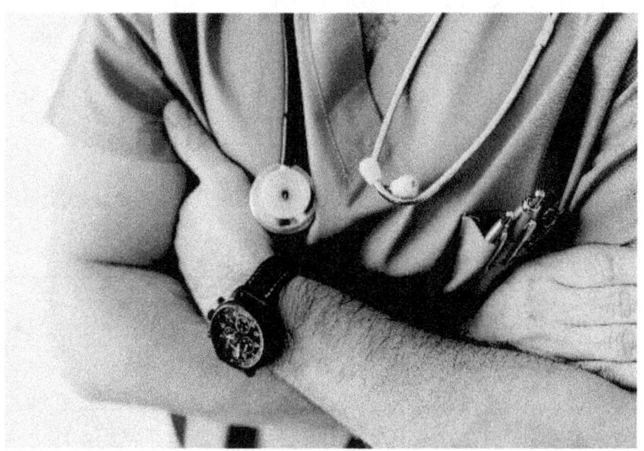

Exercise 1- Draw a line connecting each word to its correct definition.

Word	Meaning
Insurance	A scheduled meeting with a healthcare provider
Prescription	A recommendation to see another doctor or specialist
Specialist	Basic health services provided by general doctors
Referral	A written order from a healthcare provider for medicine
Co-payment	A hospital area for urgent and severe health issues
Appointment	A system for protecting against financial loss
Primary Care	A doctor who focuses on a specific area of medicine
Emergency Room	A small fee paid by the patient at each visit to the healthcare provider

Exercise 2- Read the text below before answering the questions.

Navigating the Healthcare System

The US healthcare system can be complex, with various options for receiving care. Primary care doctors are often the first point of contact for patients. They provide general health services, manage chronic illnesses, and refer patients to specialists when needed. For example, if a patient needs eye care, the primary care doctor may refer them to an eye doctor or ophthalmologist.

In addition to primary care, patients may need to visit specialists for specific health concerns. For instance, a cardiologist specializes in heart-related issues, while a dermatologist focuses on skin conditions. Patients often need a referral from their primary care doctor to see a specialist. Understanding the roles of different healthcare providers helps patients navigate the system effectively.

Comprehension Questions:

1. What is the role of a primary care doctor?

____

2. Why might a patient be referred to a specialist?

____

3. What might a primary care doctor do if a patient needs eye care?

____

4. What does a dermatologist specialize in?

____

5. Why is it important to understand the roles of different healthcare providers?

____

6. Summarize each paragraph in your own words.

____

Exercise 3- Read the text below before answering the questions.

Understanding Health Insurance

Health insurance helps cover the cost of medical services. There are various types of insurance plans, including private insurance, employer-provided insurance, and government programs like Medicaid and Medicare. Each plan has its own rules about coverage, including what services are covered and which doctors are in the network.

Patients often have to pay a co-payment when they visit a doctor. This is a small fee that is part of the cost of the visit. Insurance also typically covers prescriptions, but the patient may need to pay a portion of the cost. It's important for patients to understand their insurance plan to avoid unexpected expenses and ensure they receive the care they need.

Comprehension Questions:

1. What are two types of health insurance mentioned in the text?

____

2. What is a co-payment?

____

3. How can insurance help with the cost of prescriptions?

____

4. Why is it important to understand your insurance plan?

____

5. Name a government program that provides health insurance.

____

6. Summarize each paragraph in your own words.

____

Exercise 4- Read the text below before answering the questions.

Using Healthcare Services

Scheduling an appointment is usually the first step in receiving healthcare services. Patients can schedule appointments by phone, online, or in person. It's important to arrive on time and bring any necessary documents, such as insurance cards and medical history. In some cases, patients may need a prescription for medication, which they can get from their doctor.

In emergencies, patients should go to the emergency room, where they can receive immediate care for serious issues. The emergency room is equipped to handle urgent situations, such as severe injuries and illnesses. Knowing when to visit a primary care doctor, a specialist, or the emergency room can help patients receive the appropriate level of care.

Comprehension Questions:

1. How can patients schedule an appointment?

____

2. What should patients bring to their appointment?

____

3. Where should patients go in an emergency?

____

4. What types of situations are handled in the emergency room?

____

5. Why is it important to know the different healthcare services available?

____

6. Summarize each paragraph in your own words.

____

Catalog of Medical Services

Provider	Specialty	Schedule	Accepting New Patients	Insurance Accepted
Dr. Smith	Generalist	Mon., Wed., Fri. (9 AM - 5 PM)	Yes	All major insurance
Dr. Johnson	Dentist	Tue., Thu. (10 AM - 6 PM)	No	Private insurance only
Dr. Lee	Eye Doctor	Mon. – Fri. (8 AM - 4 PM)	Yes	Medicare, Medicaid
Dr. Martinez	Cardiologist	Wed., Thu. (9 AM - 5 PM)	Yes	Private insurance, Medicare
Dr. Patel	Dermatologist	Mon., Tue., Fri. (11 AM - 7 PM)	No	All major insurance, Medicaid

Comprehension Questions:

1. Which doctor specializes in heart-related issues?

____

2. On which days is Dr. Smith available?

____

3. Does Dr. Johnson accept new patients?

____

4. What types of insurance does Dr. Lee accept?

____

5. Can patients with Medicaid see Dr. Patel?

____

Tips on Finding a Good Primary Care Doctor

Number	Tip
1	Check if the doctor accepts your insurance.
2	Ask for recommendations from friends and family.
3	Research the doctor's credentials and experience.
4	Consider the location and office hours.
5	Meet the doctor to see if you feel comfortable.
6	Check if the doctor's office has helpful staff.
7	Ensure the doctor has hospital affiliations if needed.

Comprehension Questions:

1. Why is it important to check if the doctor accepts your insurance?

____

2. What should you consider about the doctor's office location?

____

3. Why might hospital affiliations be important?

____

4. What can you do to learn about the doctor's experience?

____

5. Why is it helpful to ask friends and family for recommendations?

____

Exercise 7- Fill in the blanks with the correct words (*insurance, referral, specialist, emergency, appointment*).

1. A _______________ is a doctor who focuses on a specific area of medicine.

2. The _______________ room is for urgent and severe health issues.

3. Patients may need a _______________ to see a specialist.

4. The _______________ helps cover the cost of medical services.

5. An _______________ is a scheduled meeting with a healthcare provider.

Exercise 8- Dictation

Your teacher will read some of the new words from Exercise 1. Write down what you hear.

____

____

Exercise 9- Writing

Write a paragraph to summarize what you know and learned about the health care system and services.

____

____

____

____

____

____

____

ANSWER KEYS

Exercise 1- Vocabulary Matching:
1. Insurance - A system for protecting against financial loss
2. Prescription - A written order from a healthcare provider for medicine
3. Specialist - A doctor who focuses on a specific area of medicine
4. Referral - A recommendation to see another doctor or specialist
5. Co-payment - A small fee paid by the patient at each visit to the healthcare provider
6. Appointment - A scheduled meeting with a healthcare provider
7. Primary Care - Basic health services provided by general doctors
8. Emergency Room - A hospital area for urgent and severe health issues

Exercise 2- Text 1:
1. A primary care doctor provides general health services, manages illnesses and refers patients to specialists.
2. A patient might be referred to a specialist for specific health concerns.
3. They may refer the patient to an eye doctor or ophthalmologist.
4. A dermatologist specializes in skin conditions.
5. Understanding the roles helps patients navigate the healthcare system effectively.
6. Paragraph 1: Primary care doctors are the first point of contact for patients, offering general services and referrals to specialists if needed.
   Paragraph 2: Specialists address specific health issues and often require a referral from a primary care doctor. Understanding their roles aids in navigating the healthcare system.

Exercise 3- Text 2:
1. Two types of health insurance are private insurance and government programs.
2. A co-payment is a small fee paid by the patient at each visit.
3. Insurance helps by covering a portion of the cost.
4. It is important for patients to understand so they can avoid unexpected expenses and ensure they receive the care they need.
5. Medicaid is one example of a government program.
6. Paragraph 1: Health insurance covers medical costs, with private, employer-provided, and government plans offering different coverage.

Paragraph 2: Patients pay co-pays, and insurance helps with prescriptions. Know your plan to avoid extra costs.

Exercise 4- Text 3:
1. Patients can schedule an appointment by phone, online, or in person.
2. Patients should bring necessary documents like insurance cards and their medical history.
3. They should go to the emergency room.
4. Severe injuries and illnesses are handled in the emergency room.
5. It is important to know to receive the appropriate level of care.
6. Paragraph 1: Patients can schedule appointments through various methods and should bring necessary documents to their appointments.
   Paragraph 2: In emergencies, patients should go to the emergency room for urgent care, and knowing the right healthcare service ensures proper treatment.

Exercise 5- Catalog of Medical Services:
1. Dr. Martinez, the cardiologist, specializes in heart-related issues.
2. Dr. Smith is available on Monday, Wednesday, and Friday.
3. No, Dr. Johnson is not accepting new patients.
4. Dr. Lee accepts Medicare and Medicaid.
5. Yes, they can see Dr. Patel.

Exercise 6- Tips on Finding a Good Primary Care Doctor:
1. It ensures that your medical costs will be covered.
2. You should consider if the location is convenient for you.
3. Hospital affiliations are important in case you need hospital visits or care.
4. You can find out online or through medical boards.
5. They may provide trusted and valuable suggestions based on personal experiences.

Exercise 7- Fill-in-the-Blanks:
1. Specialist
2. Emergency
3. Referral
4. Insurance
5. Appointment

Lesson 2: Safety Measures and Health Risks

Objectives for the Lesson:

- Students will learn key vocabulary related to safety measures and health risks.

- Students will read and answer questions on the importance of health safety and precautionary measures in daily life.

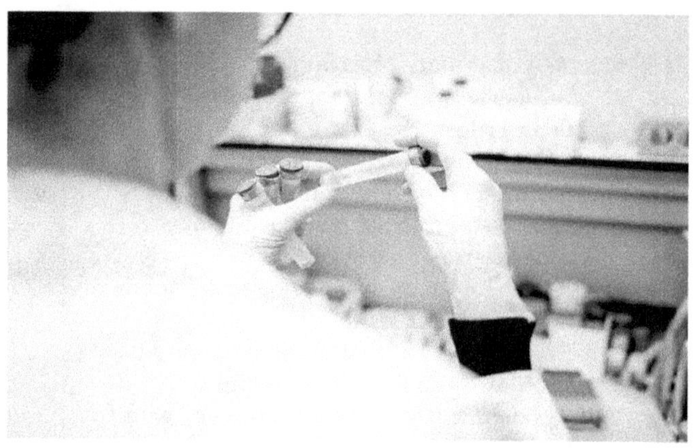

Exercise 1- Draw a line connecting each word to its correct definition.

Word	Meaning
Precaution	Signs of physical and mental illness
Hygiene	A potential source of danger
Immunization	The presence of harmful substances
Symptoms	An action taken to prevent harm
Infection	Immediate help given to a person who is injured or suddenly sick
Hazard	Practices that maintain cleanliness
First Aid	The invasion of harmful microorganisms in the body
Contamination	The process of receiving a vaccine to protect against diseases

Exercise 2- Read the text below before answering the questions.

Importance of Hygiene

Maintaining good hygiene is essential for preventing illnesses. Personal hygiene includes daily habits like brushing teeth and bathing, which help remove harmful bacteria from the body. Simple actions like washing hands regularly can significantly reduce the spread of infections. Using hand sanitizers when soap and water are unavailable is also effective.

In workplaces, maintaining hygiene can prevent the spread of germs. Employers often provide hand sanitizers and encourage employees to clean their workspaces. Good hygiene practices are crucial, especially during flu season, to protect oneself and others. Understanding the importance of hygiene helps create a healthier environment.

Comprehension Questions:

1. Why is maintaining good hygiene important?

____

2. What can reduce the spread of infections?

____

3. What are two examples of personal hygiene?

____

4. Why is workplace hygiene important?

____

5. When is it especially crucial to practice good hygiene?

____

6. Summarize each paragraph in your own words.

____

Exercise 3- Read the text below before answering the questions.

Understanding Health Risks

Health risks can arise from various sources, including environmental hazards and unhealthy behaviors. Smoking, for example, increases the risk of lung cancer and other diseases. Exposure to harmful chemicals at work can also pose health risks. It is essential to recognize these risks and take preventive measures.

Employers are responsible for ensuring a safe work environment by providing proper safety equipment and training. Employees should also be aware of the risks associated with their jobs and follow safety protocols. By understanding and managing health risks, individuals can protect their well-being and prevent accidents.

Comprehension Questions:

1. What are two sources of health risks mentioned in the text?

____

2. How can smoking affect health?

____

3. What is the role of employers in managing health risks?

____

4. What should employees do to stay safe at work?

____

5. Why is it important to manage health risks?

____

6. Summarize each paragraph in your own words.

____

Preventing Infections

Infections can spread through various means, including physical contact and airborne particles. Vaccination is a critical method of preventing infectious diseases. Immunizations help the body develop immunity to specific infections, reducing the likelihood of contracting them. Common vaccines include those for flu, measles, and hepatitis.

Practicing good hygiene, such as covering your mouth when coughing and washing your hands, can prevent the spread of infections. In case of illness, it is advisable to stay home and avoid close contact with others. These preventive measures are essential in controlling the spread of infectious diseases and protecting public health.

Comprehension Questions:

1. How can infections spread?

____

2. What is the purpose of vaccination?

____

3. Name three common vaccines mentioned in the text.

____

4. What should you do if you are ill to prevent spreading infection?

____

5. Why are preventive measures important?

____

6. Summarize each paragraph in your own words.

____

Email from BKT Company HR Director

From:	HRDirector@BKTCompany.com
To:	AllStaff@BKTCompany.com
Subject:	Health Safety and Precautions During Flu Season

Dear Staff,

As we enter the flu season, it is essential to maintain a healthy workplace. We encourage everyone to get vaccinated and practice good hygiene, such as frequent handwashing and using hand sanitizers. If you feel unwell, please stay home and consult a healthcare provider. Remember to clean your workspace regularly and avoid close contact with sick individuals. Together, we can keep our workplace safe and healthy.

Sincerely,

HR Director

Comprehension Questions:

1. What is the main purpose of the email?

____

2. What are two hygiene practices mentioned?

____

3. What should employees do if they feel unwell?

____

4. Who sent the email?

____

5. Why is it important to avoid close contact with sick individuals?

____

Tips to Avoid Health Risks

Number	Tip
1	Wash hands frequently.
2	Get vaccinated.
3	Avoid touching your face.
4	Eat a balanced diet.
5	Exercise regularly.
6	Avoid smoking and excessive alcohol consumption.
7	Use safety equipment at work.
8	Stay hydrated.
9	Get regular medical check-ups.
10	Practice safe food handling.

Comprehension Questions:

1. What is the first tip mentioned on the poster?

____

2. Why is it important to eat a balanced diet?

____

3. What should you avoid to reduce health risks?

____

4. Why is staying hydrated important?

____

5. How can regular medical check-ups help?

____

Exercise 7- Fill in the blanks with the correct words (*vaccinated, hazard, hygiene, close, safety*).

1. It is important to practice good _______________ to prevent infections.

2. Getting _______________ helps protect against diseases like flu and measles.

3. A _______________ can result from exposure to dangerous chemicals.

4. Employers should provide proper _______________ equipment at work.

5. Avoid _______________ contact with sick individuals to prevent spreading illness.

Exercise 8- Dictation

Your teacher will read some of the new words from Exercise 1. Write down what you hear.

____

____

Exercise 9- Writing

Write a paragraph to summarize what you know and learned about safety measures and health risks.

____

____

____

____

____

____

____

ANSWER KEYS

Exercise 1- Vocabulary Matching:
1. Precaution - An action taken to prevent harm
2. Hygiene - Practices that maintain cleanliness
3. Immunization - The process of receiving a vaccine to protect against diseases.
4. Symptoms - Signs of physical and mental illness
5. Infection - The invasion of harmful microorganisms in the body
6. Hazard - A potential source of danger
7. First Aid - Immediate help given to a person who is injured or suddenly sick
8. Contamination - The presence of harmful substances

Exercise 2- Text 1:
1. Maintaining good hygiene is important for preventing illnesses.
2. Washing hands regularly and using hand sanitizers can reduce the spread of infections.
3. Brushing teeth and bathing are examples of personal hygiene.
4. Workplace hygiene is important to prevent the spread of germs among employees.
5. It is especially crucial to practice good hygiene during flu season.
6. Paragraph 1: Good hygiene practices like brushing teeth, bathing, and washing hands are essential for preventing illnesses and infections.
   Paragraph 2: In workplaces, maintaining hygiene helps prevent the spread of germs, especially during flu season, contributing to a healthier environment.

Exercise 3- Text 2:
1. Environmental hazards and unhealthy behaviors are two sources of health risks.
2. Smoking increases the risk of lung cancer.
3. Employers are responsible for ensuring a safe work environment by providing proper safety equipment and training.
4. Employees should be aware of the risks associated with their jobs and follow safety protocols.
5. It is important to protect well-being and prevent accidents
6. Paragraph 1: Health risks can come from unhealthy habits, and it is important to recognize and address these risks.
   Paragraph 2: Employers must provide a safe work environment, and employees should follow safety guidelines to avoid accidents and maintain their health.

Exercise 4- Text 3:
1. Infections can spread through physical contact and airborne particles.
2. Vaccination helps the body develop immunity to infections.
3. Flu, measles, hepatitis vaccines are mentioned.
4. Stay home and avoid close contact with others
5. Preventive measures are important for controlling the spread of infectious diseases and protecting public health.
6. Paragraph 1: Infections spread through contact and airborne particles. Vaccination is key for developing immunity against diseases like flu, measles, and hepatitis.
   Paragraph 2: Good hygiene practices and staying home when ill help prevent the spread of infections, which is crucial for public health.

Exercise 5- Email from BKT Company HR Director
1. The main purpose is to encourage health safety and precautions during flu season
2. Frequent handwashing and using hand sanitizers are mentioned.
3. Employees should stay home and consult a healthcare provider.
4. The email was sent by the HR Director of BKT Company.
5. It is important to avoid close contact to prevent spreading illnesses.

Exercise 6: Tips to Avoid Health Risks
1. The first tip is to wash hands frequently.
2. Eating a balanced diet is important for overall health and prevents health issues.
3. You should avoid smoking and excessive alcohol consumption.
4. Staying hydrated helps maintain bodily functions and overall health.
5. They help detect health issues early.

Exercise 7- Fill-in-the-Blanks:
1. hygiene
2. vaccinated
3. hazard
4. safety
5. close

Lesson 3: Health Maintenance and Prevention

Objectives for the Lesson:

- Students will learn key vocabulary related to health maintenance and prevention.

- Students will read and answer questions on the importance of preventive care and healthy habits.

Exercise 1- Draw a line connecting each word to its correct definition.

Word	Meaning
Nutrition	Actions taken to reduce the risk of illness or injury
Exercise	Mental or emotional tension
Screening	Practices for cleanliness and health
Hydration	A routine medical examination
Hygiene	The act of drinking enough fluids, mainly water
Stress	Physical activity for fitness and health
Check-up	Tests to detect potential health issues
Prevention	The process of obtaining and utilizing nutrients from food

Exercise 2- Read the text below before answering the questions.

The Importance of Nutrition

Good nutrition is a key aspect of maintaining health. Eating a balanced diet with plenty of fruits, vegetables, and whole grains provides the body with essential nutrients. These nutrients support bodily functions and prevent illnesses. For example, vitamin C found in citrus fruits helps boost the immune system.

In addition to a healthy diet, staying hydrated is also important. Drinking enough water daily helps maintain bodily functions and keeps the body hydrated. It is recommended to drink at least eight glasses of water a day. Proper nutrition and hydration are foundational for good health and wellness.

Comprehension Questions:

1. What is an example of a food group that is important for nutrition?

____

2. How does vitamin C benefit the body?

____

3. Why is drinking enough water important?

____

4. How many glasses of water should one drink daily?

____

5. What are two key components of good nutrition?

____

6. Summarize each paragraph in your own words.

____

Exercise 3- Read the text below before answering the questions.

The Role of Exercise in Health Maintenance

Regular exercise is crucial for maintaining a healthy body. Physical activities like walking, running, or swimming help keep the heart strong and muscles flexible. Exercise also helps manage weight, which can reduce the risk of chronic diseases like diabetes and heart disease. Engaging in regular physical activity improves overall fitness and well-being.

Moreover, exercise has mental health benefits. It can reduce stress and improve mood by releasing endorphins, which are natural mood lifters. Even simple activities like stretching or a short walk can make a difference. Making time for regular exercise is an essential part of a healthy lifestyle.

Comprehension Questions:

1. What are three examples of physical activities mentioned in the text?

____

2. How does exercise benefit the heart?

____

3. What can regular exercise help prevent?

____

4. How do endorphins affect mood?

____

5. Why is it important to include exercise in one's routine?

____

6. Summarize each paragraph in your own words.

____

Exercise 4- Read the text below before answering the questions.

Preventive Care and Health Check-ups

Preventive care involves taking steps to prevent illnesses before they occur. This includes regular health check-ups and screenings. Visiting a doctor for routine check-ups helps detect potential health issues early. Early detection can lead to better treatment outcomes and prevent complications.

Immunizations are another important aspect of preventive care. Vaccines protect against diseases like the flu, measles, and pneumonia. Staying up-to-date with vaccinations can prevent the spread of infectious diseases. Preventive care, including regular check-ups and vaccinations, is essential for maintaining good health.

Comprehension Questions:

1. What is the purpose of preventive care?

____

2. Why are regular health check-ups important?

____

3. Name three diseases that vaccines can protect against.

____

4. What is the benefit of early detection of health issues?

____

5. How does preventive care contribute to overall health?

____

6. Summarize each paragraph in your own words.

____

Important Healthy Habits for Preventive Care

Healthy Habits	
1	Eat a balanced diet.
2	Stay physically active.
3	Get regular health check-ups.
4	Stay hydrated.
5	Get enough sleep.
6	Practice good hygiene.
7	Manage stress effectively.
8	Avoid smoking and excessive alcohol.
9	Stay up to date with vaccinations.

Comprehension Questions:

1. What is the first habit mentioned on the poster?

____

2. Why is staying physically active important?

____

3. How does getting enough sleep contribute to health?

____

4. What should one avoid to maintain good health?

____

5. Why are vaccinations important?

____

Exercise 6- Fill in the blanks with the correct words (infectious, vegetables, stress, hygiene, exercise)

1. A balanced diet includes plenty of fruits and _______________.

2. Regular _______________ helps keep the heart strong.

3. Immunizations protect against _______________ diseases.

4. _______________ is important for maintaining cleanliness.

5. Managing _______________ can improve mental well-being.

Exercise 7- Dictation

Your teacher will read some of the new words from Exercise 1. Write down what you hear.

____

____

Exercise 8- Writing

Write a paragraph to summarize what you know and learned about health maintenance and prevention.

Answer Keys

Exercise 1- Vocabulary Matching:
1. Nutrition - The process of obtaining and utilizing nutrients from food
2. Exercise - Physical activity for fitness and health
3. Screening - Tests to detect potential health issues
4. Hydration - The act of drinking enough fluids, mainly water
5. Hygiene - Practices for cleanliness and health
6. Stress - Mental or emotional tension
7. Check-up - A routine medical examination
8. Prevention - Actions taken to reduce the risk of illness or injury

Exercise 2- Text 1:
1. Fruits, vegetables, and whole grains are important.
2. Vitamin C boosts the immune system.
3. Drinking water helps maintain bodily functions and keeps the body hydrated.
4. One should drink at least eight glasses of water.
5. A balanced diet and staying hydrated are two key components.
6. Paragraph 1: Good nutrition includes eating fruits, vegetables, and whole grains to get essential nutrients.
   Paragraph 2: Staying hydrated by drinking at least eight glasses of water daily supports bodily functions and overall health.

Exercise 3- Text 2:
1. Examples of physical activities are walking, running, and swimming.
2. Exercise keeps the heart strong.
3. Regular exercise can help prevent chronic diseases like diabetes and heart disease.
4. Endorphins are mood lifters that reduce stress and improve overall mood.
5. Exercise improves overall fitness, well-being, and mental health, and helps prevent chronic diseases.

6. Paragraph 1: Regular exercise keeps the body healthy by strengthening the heart, maintaining muscle flexibility, managing weight, and reducing the risk of chronic diseases.
   Paragraph 2: Exercise benefits mental health by releasing endorphins that reduce stress and improve mood.

Exercise 4- Text 3:
1. Preventive care avoids illnesses before they occur.
2. Regular health check-ups detect potential health issues early.
3. Vaccines can protect against the flu, measles, and pneumonia.
4. Early detection leads to better treatment outcomes and helps prevent complications.
5. Preventive care prevents diseases and manages health risks.
6. Paragraph 1: Preventive care involves actions like regular check-ups to detect and prevent illnesses before they worsen.
   Paragraph 2: Vaccinations are a key part of preventive care, protecting against diseases and preventing their spread.

Exercise 5- Important Healthy Habits for Preventive Care
1. The first habit mentioned is eating a balanced diet
2. Staying active helps maintain physical health and fitness.
3. Getting enough sleep restores the body and mind.
4. One should avoid smoking and excessive alcohol.
5. Vaccinations protect against infectious diseases.

Exercise 6- Fill-in-the-Blanks:
1. vegetables
2. exercise
3. infectious
4. hygiene
5. stress

Lesson 4: Health and Medical Information

Objectives for the Lesson:

- Students will learn key vocabulary and basic concepts used in medical contexts.

- Students read and answer questions related to health and medical information.

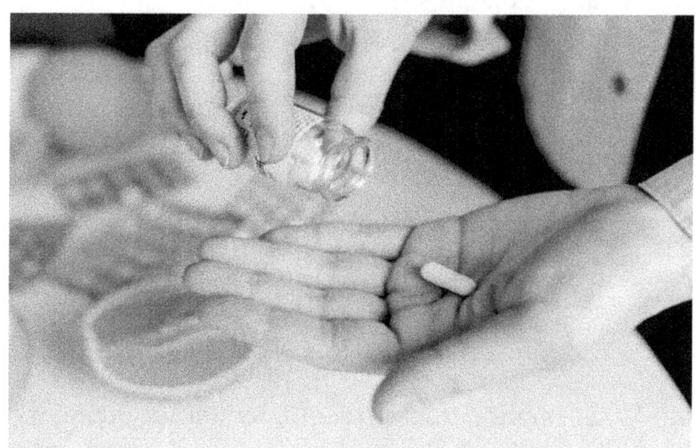

Exercise 1- Draw a line connecting each word to its correct definition.

Word	Meaning
Diagnosis	The care given to a patient for an illness or injury
Pharmacist	A drug or medicine used to treat an illness
Surgery	The process of getting better after illness or injury
Treatment	The signs of illness or injury
Dosage	The amount of medicine to take at one time
Symptoms	A healthcare professional who dispenses medication
Medication	The identification of a disease
Recovery	A medical operation

Exercise 2- Read the text below before answering the questions.

Understanding a Diagnosis

When visiting a doctor, receiving a diagnosis is the first step to understanding your health condition. A diagnosis identifies what illness or medical issue you may have. For example, if you are diagnosed with diabetes, it means your blood sugar levels are too high. The doctor will explain the diagnosis and recommend steps to manage your condition.

Understanding your diagnosis is important because it helps you take the right steps toward recovery. Doctors may recommend lifestyle changes, medications, or further tests. It is essential to ask questions and understand all the information provided by the doctor. Being informed about your diagnosis can help you make better health decisions.

Comprehension Questions:

1. What is a diagnosis?

____

2. What does it mean if someone is diagnosed with diabetes?

____

3. Why is understanding a diagnosis important?

____

4. What might a doctor recommend after giving a diagnosis?

____

5. What should patients do if they do not understand the information provided?

____

6. Summarize each paragraph in your own words.

____

Exercise 3- Read the text below before answering the questions.

The Role of Medication in Treatment

Medications are often prescribed as part of a treatment plan. A prescription is a written order from a doctor that allows you to get specific medicine. The medication can help manage symptoms, cure an illness, or prevent complications. It is crucial to follow the doctor's instructions on how to take the medicine.

The dosage of medication is the amount you need to take. It is important to take the correct dosage at the right times. If you take too little, the medicine may not work; if you take too much, it could be harmful. Always follow the prescription details and ask your pharmacist if you have any questions.

Comprehension Questions:

1. What is a prescription?

____

2. Why is it important to follow the doctor's instructions for medication?

____

3. What could happen if you take the wrong dosage?

____

4. Who should you ask if you have questions about your medication?

____

5. What are two purposes of medication mentioned in the text?

____

6. Summarize each paragraph in your own words.

____

Exercise 4- Read the text below before answering the questions.

Preparing for Surgery

Surgery is sometimes necessary to treat a medical condition. It involves an operation performed by a surgeon. Before surgery, patients often receive detailed instructions on how to prepare. This may include not eating or drinking for several hours before the procedure. It is also important to inform the medical team about any allergies or medications you are taking.

After surgery, patients need time to recover. The recovery process may involve rest, medication, and follow-up appointments. It is important to follow all post-surgery care instructions to ensure a smooth recovery. Understanding the surgery process and recovery plan can help reduce anxiety and promote healing.

Comprehension Questions:

1. What is surgery?

____

2. Why is it important to inform the medical team about allergies?

____

3. What might patients need to do before surgery?

____

4. What is involved in the recovery process after surgery?

____

5. How can understanding the surgery process help patients?

____

6. Summarize each paragraph in your own words.

____

Exercise 5- Read the letter below before answering the questions.

Letter from Dr. Dialo to Julie:

Dear Julie,

After reviewing your medical tests, I have diagnosed you with gallstones. This condition occurs when hard particles form in the gallbladder. To treat this, I recommend a surgical procedure called cholecystectomy, where the gallbladder is removed.

The surgery is usually safe and can help prevent further complications. You will need to fast for at least 8 hours before the surgery. After the operation, you will be prescribed pain medication. The typical dosage is one tablet every 6 hours as needed for pain. It is important to follow all post-surgery instructions for a smooth recovery.

Please feel free to ask any questions about the surgery or recovery process.

Sincerely,

Dr. Dialo

Comprehension Questions:

1. What medical condition does Julie have?

____

2. What is the recommended treatment for Julie's condition?

____

3. How long should Julie fast before the surgery?

____

4. What medication will Julie be prescribed after the surgery?

____

5. Why is it important for Julie to follow post-surgery instructions?

____

6. Summarize the letter in your own words.

____

Exercise 6- Fill in the blanks with the correct words (*prescription, symptoms, dosage, follow, recovery, surgery*).

1. A _______________ is a doctor's order for medicine.

2. The _______________ describes how much medicine to take at one time.

3. _______________ is the process of getting better after being sick.

4. _______________ are signs that something is wrong in the body.

5. _______________ is a medical operation performed by a surgeon.

6. It is important to _______________ the doctor's instructions carefully.

Exercise 7- Dictation

Your teacher will read some of the new words from Exercise 1. Write down what you hear.

____

____

Exercise 8- Writing

Write a paragraph to summarize what you know and learned about health and medical information.

____

____

____

____

____

____

ANSWER KEYS

Exercise 1- Vocabulary Matching:
1. Diagnosis - The identification of a disease
2. Pharmacist- A healthcare professional who dispenses medication
3. Surgery - A medical operation
4. Treatment - The care given to a patient for an illness or injury
5. Dosage - The amount of medicine to take at one time
6. Symptoms - The signs of illness or injury
7. Medication – A drug or medicine used to treat an illness
8. Recovery - The process of getting better after illness or injury

Exercise 2- Text 1:
1. A diagnosis is the identification of a disease or condition.
2. It means they have high blood sugar levels.
3. Understanding a diagnosis helps individuals take the right steps toward recovery and make informed health decisions.
4. A doctor might recommend lifestyle changes, medications, or further tests.
5. Patients should ask questions and seek clarification.
6. Paragraph 1: A diagnosis identifies your health condition and how to manage it, like treating diabetes.
Paragraph 2: Understanding your diagnosis helps you take proper steps for recovery and make informed decisions.

Exercise 3- Text 2:
1. A prescription is a doctor's written order for medicine.
2. Following the instructions ensures the medicine works and is safe.
3. Taking too little might not be effective, while taking too much could be harmful.
4. You should ask your pharmacist.
5. Medications can manage symptoms, cure illness, or prevent complications.
6. Paragraph 1: A prescription is a doctor's order for medicine that helps manage or cure conditions.

Paragraph 2: It is crucial to take the correct dosage as directed to avoid ineffectiveness or harm.

Exercise 4- Text 3:
1. Surgery is a medical operation.
2. It is important to prevent allergic reactions.
3. Patients might need to fast for several hours before surgery.
4. Recovery includes rest, medication, and follow-up appointments.
5. It can reduce anxiety and promote healing.
6. Paragraph 1 Summary: Surgery is an operation needed to treat conditions, with preparation instructions including fasting and disclosing allergies.
Paragraph 2 Summary: Post-surgery recovery involves rest, medication, and follow-up care. Knowing the process helps with healing and reduces anxiety.

Exercise 5- Letter from Dr. Dialo to Julie:
1. Julie has gallstones.
2. The recommended treatment is cholecystectomy to remove the gallbladder.
3. Julie should fast for at least 8 hours.
4. Julie will be prescribed pain medication, one tablet every 6 hours as needed.
5. Following the instructions will ensure a smooth recovery and prevent complications.
6. Dr. Dialo has diagnosed Julie with gallstones and recommends surgery to remove her gallbladder. Julie needs to fast for 8 hours before the surgery and will be given pain medication afterward. It's crucial for her to follow post-surgery instructions for a good recovery.

Exercise 6- Fill-in-the-Blanks:
1. Prescription
2. Dosage
3. Recovery
4. Symptoms
5. Surgery
6. Follow

REFLECTION ON LEARNING

Answer the following questions and discuss your responses with your teacher or classmates.

1. What reading strategies did you learn or practice in this unit?

2. What new concepts or words did you learn?

3. What reading challenges did you face?

4. What reading strategies do you need to improve?

5. What do you want your teacher to know?

UNIT 4: EMPLOYMENT

Lesson 1: Getting A Job

Objectives for the Lesson:

- Students will learn and use essential vocabulary related to job searching and employment.

- Students will read and answer questions on the basic strategies for finding a job.

Exercise 1- Draw a line connecting each word to its correct definition.

Word	Meaning
Resume	A letter explaining why you want the job
Interview	A form filled out to apply for a job
Networking	To offer your time and skills without getting paid
Application	A meeting where questions are asked for a job
Vacancy	A document listing work experience and skills
Reference	A person who can speak about your abilities
Cover Letter	An open position that needs to be filled
Volunteer	Meeting people to share information and contacts

Exercise 2- Read the text below before answering the questions.

The Importance of a Resume

A resume is a crucial tool in the job search process. It is a document that lists your work experience, skills, and education. Employers use resumes to learn about potential employees. A well-organized resume can make a strong impression and increase your chances of getting an interview. Creating a good resume involves highlighting your strengths. It should be clear and concise, with accurate information. Tailoring your resume to the job you are applying for is also important. This means you should adjust your resume to match the skills and experience the employer is looking for. Always proofread your resume to avoid mistakes.

Comprehension Questions:

1. What is a resume?

____

2. Why do employers use resumes?

____

3. How can a well-organized resume help you?

____

4. What should you include in your resume?

____

5. Why is it important to tailor your resume to the job?

____

6. What should you do before sending your resume?

____

7. What questions do you have about writing a resume?

____

Exercise 3- Read the text below before answering the questions.

Networking and Its Benefits

Networking is the process of meeting people and sharing information. It is an important aspect of finding a job. Many jobs are not advertised, so knowing people in your industry can help you learn about these opportunities. Networking can be done at events, through friends, or on social media.

Building a professional network can provide support and advice. It allows you to connect with others who can help you in your job search. When networking, it is important to be polite and professional. You should always be ready to share information about your skills and experience.

Comprehension Questions:

1. What is networking?

2. Why is networking important in finding a job?

3. How can you network?

4. What are some benefits of having a professional network?

5. How should you behave when networking?

6. What should you share when networking?

7. What questions do you have about networking?

Exercise 4- Read the text below before answering the questions.

Using the Internet for Job Searching

The Internet is a powerful tool for finding jobs. Many companies post job openings online. Websites like LinkedIn and Indeed allow you to search for jobs by location and industry. You can also set up alerts to notify you when new jobs are posted.

Applying for jobs online is often quick and easy. You can upload your resume and cover letter directly to the company's website. It is important to follow the instructions carefully when applying online. This includes filling out all required fields and attaching the necessary documents. Always double-check the information before submitting your application.

Comprehension Questions:

1. How can the Internet help you find a job?

2. What are some websites where you can search for jobs?

____

3. What is an advantage of applying for jobs online?

____

4. What should you do when applying for jobs online?

____

5. Why is it important to follow instructions when applying online?

____

6. What should you do before submitting an online application?

____

7. What questions do you have about job search?

____

Exercise 5- Read the interview techniques below before answering the questions.

Interview Techniques
1. Dress professionally.
2. Arrive on time.
3. Research the company.
4. Prepare answers to common questions.
5. Bring copies of your resume.
6. Be polite and respectful.
7. Ask questions about the job.

Comprehension Questions:

1. What should you wear to an interview?

____

2. Why is it important to arrive on time?

____

3.   How can researching the company help you in an interview?

____

4.   What should you bring to the interview?

____

5.   Why should you ask questions during the interview?

____

Exercise 6- Read the job search strategies below before answering the questions.

Online Job Search Strategies Checklist	
	Create a professional profile on LinkedIn.
	Use job search websites like Indeed.
	Set up email alerts for new job postings.
	Customize your resume for each application.
	Network with professionals on social media.
	Follow companies you're interested in.
	Research the company's website.
	Keep track of the jobs you've applied for.

Comprehension Questions:

1.   Why should you create a professional profile on LinkedIn?

____

2.   How can job search websites help you?

____

3.   What is the benefit of setting up email alerts?

____

4.   Why should you customize your resume for each job?

____

5.   How can you keep track of the jobs you've applied for?

____

Exercise 7- Fill in the blanks with the correct words (*networking, cover letter, resume, vacancy, volunteer*).

1. A _______________ is a document listing work experience and skills.

2. _______________ is meeting people to share information and contacts.

3. An _______________ is a form filled out to apply for a job.

4. A _______________ explains why you want the job.

5. To _______________ means to offer your time and skills without getting paid

6. A _______________ is an open position that needs to be filled.

Exercise 8- Dictation

Your teacher will read some of the new words from Exercise 1. Write down what you hear.

____

____

Exercise 9- Writing

Write a paragraph to summarize what you know and learned about job searching and employment.

____

____

____

____

____

____

ANSWER KEYS

Exercise 1- Vocabulary Matching:
1. Resume - A document listing work experience and skills
2. Interview - A meeting where questions are asked for a job
3. Networking - Meeting people to share information and contacts
4. Application - A form filled out to apply for a job
5. Vacancy - An open position that needs to be filled
6. Reference - A person who can speak about your abilities
7. Cover Letter - A letter explaining why you want the job
8. Volunteer - To offer your time and skills without getting paid

Exercise 2- Text 1:
1. A resume is a document listing work experience, skills, and education.
2. Employers use resumes to learn about potential employees.
3. A well-organized resume increases your chances of getting an interview.
4. You should include your work experience, skills, and education.
5. It is important to match the employer's needs.
6. You should proofread your resume to avoid mistakes.

Exercise 3- Text 2:
1. Networking is the process of meeting people and sharing information.
2. It helps you learn about job opportunities as many jobs are not advertised.
3. You can network at events, through friends, or on social media.
4. A professional network can provide support, advice and connections.
5. You should be polite and professional.
6. You should share information about your skills and experience.

Exercise 4- Text 3:
1. The Internet gives you access to job openings posted online by companies.
2. LinkedIn and Indeed are two websites.
3. Applying online is often a quick and easy application process.
4. You should follow instructions carefully fill out all required fields, and attach the necessary documents.
5. It is important to ensure your application is complete and considered for the job.
6. You should double-check the information.

Exercise 5- Interview Techniques:
1. You should dress professionally.
2. It shows respect for the interviewer's time.
3. Researching the company helps you answer questions and show interest.
4. You should bring copies of your resume.
5. You should ask questions to show your interest and learn more about the company.

Exercise 6- Online Job Search Strategies:
1. LinkedIn helps you connect with potential employers and showcase your skills and experience.
2. Job search websites can help you find job listings in your field.
3. Alerts keep you updated on new job opportunities so you can apply promptly.
4. This helps you highlight your most relevant skills and experience that match the specific job requirements.
5. You can keep track of the jobs you've applied for by maintaining a list or spreadsheet that includes the company names, job titles, and application dates.

Exercise 7- Fill-in-the-Blanks:
1. Resume
2. Networking
3. Application
4. Cover Letter
5. Volunteer
6. Vacancy

Lesson 2: Job Safety Standards And Procedures

Objectives for the Lesson:

- Students will learn and use essential vocabulary related to workplace safety.

- Students will read and answer questions on safety standards and procedures in a work environment.

Exercise 1- Draw a line connecting each word to its correct definition.

Word	Meaning
Hazard	Designing a workplace to fit the needs and comfort of workers
PPE	A device used to put out fires
Emergency Exit	A practice exercise for emergency situations
Ergonomics	Something dangerous or risky
Safety Drill	A way out in case of an emergency
Fire Extinguisher	Personal Protective Equipment
First Aid Kit	The act of following rules and regulations
Compliance	A set of supplies for medical treatment

Exercise 2- Read the text below before answering the questions.

Understanding Workplace Hazards

Workplace hazards are potential sources of danger or harm in a work environment. Hazards can be physical, like slippery floors, or chemical, such as harmful substances. It's important for employees to be aware of these hazards to prevent accidents. Employers must also provide training and equipment to help employees stay safe.

One common hazard is electrical equipment. Faulty wiring or overloaded circuits can cause fires. Employees should know where the circuit breakers are located and how to use them safely. Proper maintenance of equipment can reduce the risk of electrical hazards. It's also important to report any unsafe conditions to a supervisor immediately.

Comprehension Questions:

1. What are workplace hazards?

____

2. Give an example of a physical hazard.

____

3. Why is it important for employees to be aware of hazards?

____

4. What should employees do if they find faulty wiring?

____

5. Who should be informed about unsafe conditions?

____

6. Summarize each paragraph in your own words.

____

Exercise 3- Read the text below before answering the questions.

Importance of PPE in the Workplace

Personal Protective Equipment (PPE) is essential for protecting workers from hazards. PPE includes items like gloves, goggles, helmets, and earplugs. Each type of PPE is designed to protect different parts of the body. For example, gloves protect hands from chemicals, while goggles protect eyes from debris.

Employers must provide the necessary PPE and ensure that employees know how to use it properly. Employees should always wear PPE when required and check for any damage before use. Proper use of PPE can prevent injuries and even save lives. It's also important to store PPE correctly to keep it in good condition.

Comprehension Questions:

1. What does PPE stand for?

____

2. Name two examples of PPE.

____

3. Why is it important to wear PPE?

____

4. Who is responsible for providing PPE?

____

5. How should PPE be stored?

____

6. What questions do you have about PPE?

____

Emergency Exits and Safety Drills

Emergency exits are crucial for safe evacuation during emergencies. All employees should know the location of emergency exits and how to use them. In case of a fire or other emergency, quick and calm evacuation is vital. Safety drills help prepare employees for these situations.

Regular safety drills should be conducted to practice evacuation procedures. These drills teach employees how to exit the building safely and where to assemble outside. It's important to follow instructions during drills and not to use elevators during emergencies. Knowing the location of fire extinguishers and how to use them can also be lifesaving.

Comprehension Questions:

1. What are emergency exits used for?

____

2. Why are safety drills important?

____

3. What should you not use during an emergency evacuation?

____

4. Where should employees go after evacuating the building?

____

5. What should employees know about fire extinguishers?

____

6. What questions do you have about safety drills?

____

Exercise 5- Read the text below before answering the questions.

Understanding Workplace Comfort and Safety

Workplace comfort and safety involves designing workspaces to fit the physical needs of workers. Proper measures can prevent injuries and improve comfort. For example, computer screens should be at eye level to avoid neck strain. Employees can make adjustments, like taking regular breaks to stretch.

Employers should provide workplace comfort and safety assessments to identify any risks. They can arrange tools and equipment to reduce reaching and bending. Adjustable chairs and desks can help maintain good posture. A well-designed workspace can lead to better productivity and fewer injuries.

Comprehension Questions:

1. What does workplace comfort and safety involve?

____

2. Why should computer screens be at eye level?

____

3. How can adjustable chairs help?

____

4. What should employers provide to identify workplace comfort and safety risks?

____

5. How can employers reduce the risk of reaching and bending?

____

Exercise 6- Read the checklist below before answering the questions.

Dos and Don'ts of Work-Related Safety Standards and Procedures

Dos	DON'Ts
Do wear PPE at all times.	Don't ignore safety signs.
Do report unsafe conditions immediately.	Don't use damaged equipment.
Do follow emergency procedures.	Don't block emergency exits.
Do keep your workspace clean.	Don't skip safety training.
Do use proper lifting techniques.	Don't rush through tasks.
Do take regular breaks.	Don't eat or drink in hazardous areas.
Do know the location of first-aid kits.	Don't leave spills unattended.
Do follow all safety protocols.	Don't forget to wear safety gear.
Do attend safety drills.	Don't hesitate to ask for help.
Do use tools and equipment correctly.	Don't take shortcuts.

Comprehension Questions:

1. Why should you wear PPE at all times?

   ____

2. What should you do if you see a blocked emergency exit?

   ____

3. Why is it important to keep your workspace clean?

   ____

4. What should you not do with damaged equipment?

   ____

5. Why should you attend safety drills?

   ____

6. What questions do you have about workplace safety?

   ____

Exercise 7- Fill in the blanks with the correct words (unsafe, emergency exit, PPE, first aid kit, fire extinguisher, assessments).

1. A _____________ is a device to put out fires.

2. Employers should provide _____________ to identify any risks.

3. _____________ is the equipment used to protect workers from hazards.

4. An _____________ is a way out in case of an emergency.

5. Always report _____________ conditions to a supervisor.

6. A _____________ is a set of tools for medical treatment.

Exercise 8- Dictation

Your teacher will read some of the new words from Exercise 1. Write down what you hear.

____

____

Exercise 9- Writing

Write a paragraph to summarize what you know and learned about job safety standards and procedures.

____

____

____

____

____

____

ANSWER KEYS

Exercise 1- Vocabulary Matching:
1. Hazard - Something dangerous or risky
2. PPE - Personal Protective Equipment
3. Emergency Exit - A way out in case of an emergency
4. Ergonomics - Designing a workplace to fit the needs and comfort of workers
5. Safety Drill – A practice exercise for emergency situations
6. Fire Extinguisher - A device used to put out fires
7. First Aid Kit - A set of supplies for medical treatment
8. Compliance - The act of following rules and regulations

Exercise 2- Text 1:
1. They are potential sources of danger or harm in a work environment.
2. A slippery floor is an example of a physical hazard.
3. Employees should be aware to prevent accidents and ensure their safety.
4. They should report it to a supervisor and avoid using it.
5. Unsafe conditions should be reported to a supervisor.
6. Paragraph 1: Workplace hazards are potential dangers and can be physical or chemical. Awareness and proper training are essential for safety.
   Paragraph 2: Electrical hazards, such as faulty wiring, can cause fires. Employees should know how to use circuit breakers and report unsafe conditions.

Exercise 3- Text 2:
1. PPE stands for Personal Protective Equipment.
2. Two examples are gloves and goggles.
3. It is important to protect workers from hazards and prevent injuries.
4. The employer is responsible.
5. It should be stored in a safe and clean place.

Exercise 4- Text 3:
1. Emergency exits are used for safe evacuation during emergencies.
2. They prepare employees for emergency evacuation.
3. You should not use elevators.
4. Employees should go to the assembly area.
5. Employees should know the location of fire extinguishers and how to use them.

Exercise 5- Text 4:
1. It involves designing workspaces to fit the physical needs of workers.
2. Computer screens should be at eye level to avoid neck strain.
3. Adjustable chairs can help maintain good posture.
4. Employers should provide workplace comfort and safety assessments.
5. They can arrange tools and equipment in a way that minimizes the need for these actions.

Exercise 6- Dos and Don'ts of Work-Related Safety Standards and Procedures:
1. Wearing PPE protects you from potential hazards and reduces the risk of injury.
2. You should report it immediately to ensure it is cleared.
3. This helps prevent accidents and injuries.
4. You should not use damaged equipment.
5. You should attend safety drills to be prepared for emergencies.

Exercise 7- Fill-in-the-Blanks:
1. Fire Extinguisher
2. Assessments
3. PPE
4. Emergency Exit
5. Unsafe
6. First Aid Kit

Lesson 3: Job Performance and Training

Objectives for the Lesson:

- Students will learn and use vocabulary related to job performance and training.

- Students will read and answer questions on job training and evaluating job performance.

Exercise 1- Draw a line connecting each word to its correct definition.

Word	Meaning
Training	Guidance from a more experienced person
Evaluation	The process of integrating new employees
Skills	Information given to help improve job performance
Performance	Assessing job performance
Promotion	How well a person does their job
Feedback	Abilities needed to do a job
Onboarding	Advancement to a higher job position
Mentorship	The process of learning skills for a job

Exercise 2- Read the text below before answering the questions.

The Importance of Job Training

Job training is essential for employees to learn the skills they need to perform their duties. It includes various methods such as workshops, online courses, and hands-on experience. Training helps employees stay updated with new tools and technologies. It also prepares them for new responsibilities.

In many companies, training is a continuous process. Employees may receive training throughout their careers to improve their skills. This ongoing learning helps them stay competitive and productive. Effective training programs are designed to meet the needs of both the company and the employees.

Comprehension Questions:

1. What is job training?

____

2. Name two methods of job training.

____

3. Why is continuous training important?

____

4. How does training benefit employees?

____

5. Who benefits from effective training programs?

____

Exercise 3- Read the text below before answering the questions.

Evaluating Employee Performance

Evaluation is a crucial part of the work environment. It helps employers assess how well employees are doing their jobs. Performance evaluations can be formal or informal. They often include feedback from supervisors, self-assessments, and peer reviews.

Regular evaluations provide opportunities for employees to receive constructive feedback. This feedback helps them understand their strengths and areas for improvement. Employers use evaluations to make decisions about promotions, raises, and training needs. It's important for employees to take evaluations seriously and use them as a tool for growth.

Comprehension Questions:

1. What is the purpose of performance evaluations?

____

2. Name one type of feedback included in evaluations.

____

3. How can evaluations benefit employees?

____

4. What decisions do employers make based on evaluations?

---

5. Why should employees take evaluations seriously?

---

6. Summarize each paragraph in your own words.

The Role of Mentorship in Job Performance

Mentorship plays a significant role in job performance and career development. A mentor is an experienced professional who provides guidance and support to a less experienced employee. Mentors help mentees navigate challenges in their job and career. They share their knowledge and experience, which can be invaluable for career growth.

Mentorship relationships can be formal or informal. Formal mentorship programs are often organized by companies, while informal mentorships develop naturally. The benefits of mentorship include increased job satisfaction, improved skills, and better understanding of the workplace. Both mentors and mentees can learn and grow from this relationship.

Comprehension Questions:

1. What is a mentor?

---

2. How do mentors help their mentees?

---

3. Can mentorship relationships be informal?

---

4. What are some benefits of mentorship?

---

5. Who can learn and grow from a mentorship relationship?

---

6. Summarize each paragraph in your own words.

____

Receiving and Using Feedback

Feedback is an essential part of job performance and improvement. It includes comments and suggestions from supervisors, peers, and even customers. Feedback can be positive, reinforcing good performance, or constructive, offering suggestions for improvement. It's important for employees to receive feedback openly and use it to enhance their work.

Constructive feedback helps employees understand what they can do better. It's a valuable tool for professional growth. Employers should provide regular feedback to help employees stay on track. Employees should also seek feedback actively and apply it to their daily tasks.

Comprehension Questions:

1. What is feedback in a work context?

____

2. What types of feedback can employees receive?

____

3. Why is it important to receive feedback openly?

____

4. How can constructive feedback help employees?

____

5. Who should seek and provide feedback?

____

6. Summarize each paragraph in your own words.

____

Incidents Related to Job Performance and Training

1. **Incident 1:** Jane received her first performance evaluation at the new job. Her supervisor praised her teamwork skills but noted that she needs to improve her time management.

> 2. **Incident 2:** During a training session, Mark learned about new software that the company would implement. He felt overwhelmed but was encouraged by his mentor, who offered additional guidance.
>
> 3. **Incident 3:** Maria attended an onboarding program where she learned about the company's safety protocols and how to use the equipment safely.

Comprehension Questions:

1. What positive feedback did Jane receive in her evaluation?

____

2. What aspect did Jane need to improve?

____

3. What new challenge did Mark face during the training session?

____

4. How did Mark's mentor support him?

____

5. What did Maria learn during the onboarding program?

____

Exercise 7- Read the strategies below before answering the questions.

> **7 Strategies for Getting a Promotion**
>
> 1. Set clear career goals.
> 2. Take on additional responsibilities.
> 3. Seek feedback and act on it.
> 4. Continue learning and improving skills.
> 5. Build strong relationships with colleagues.
> 6. Show initiative and be proactive.
> 7. Demonstrate leadership qualities.

Comprehension Questions:

1. Why is setting clear career goals important?

____

2. How can taking on additional responsibilities help in getting a promotion?

____

3. What should employees do with the feedback they receive?

____

4. Why is continuous learning important for career growth?

____

5. How can building relationships with colleagues help to get a promotion?

____

Exercise 8- Fill in the blanks with the correct words (*evaluation, PPE, mentor, promotion, training, feedback*).

1. _______________ is the process of learning skills for a job.

2. _______________ involves assessing how well someone performs their job.

3. A _______________ provides guidance and support to less experienced employees.

4. _______________ is essential for protecting workers from hazards.

5. _______________ helps employees understand their strengths and areas for improvement.

6. Taking on additional responsibilities can help in getting a _______________.

Exercise 9- Dictation

Your teacher will read some of the new words from Exercise 1. Write down what you hear.

____

____

Exercise 10- Writing

Write a paragraph to summarize what you know and learned about job performance and training..

____

____

____

____

____

ANSWER KEYS

Exercise 1- Vocabulary Matching:
1. Training - The process of learning skills for a job
2. Evaluation - Assessing job performance
3. Skills - Abilities needed to do a job
4. Performance - How well a person does their job
5. Promotion - Advancement to a higher job position
6. Feedback - Information given to help improve job performance
7. Onboarding - The process of integrating new employees
8. Mentorship - Guidance from a more experienced person

Exercise 2- Text 1:
1. Job training is the process of learning the skills to perform job duties.
2. Two methods are workshops and online courses.
3. Continuous training helps employees stay updated and competitive.
4. Training prepares them for new responsibilities and improves skills.
5. Both the company and the employees benefit.

Exercise 3- Text 2:
1. The purpose is to assess how well employees are doing their jobs.
2. One type of feedback included in evaluations is feedback from supervisors.
3. Evaluations provide opportunities for improvement.
4. Employers make decisions about promotions, raises, and training needs.
5. Employees can use them as a tool for growth and improvement.
6. Paragraph 1: Evaluations assess employee performance and can include feedback from supervisors, self-assessments, and peers.
Paragraph 2: Evaluations offer feedback to help employees improve and are used by employers to make decisions about promotions and training.

Exercise 4- Text 3:
1. A mentor is an experienced professional providing guidance.
2. Mentors help their mentees by guiding them through job challenges and sharing their knowledge and experience.
3. Yes, they can develop naturally.

4. Benefits of mentorship include increased job satisfaction, improved skills, and a better understanding of the workplace.
5. Both mentors and mentees can learn and grow.
6. Paragraph 1: Mentorship involves experienced professionals guiding less experienced employees to help with career challenges.
Paragraph 2: Mentorship can be formal or informal, leading to improved job satisfaction and skills.
Paragraph 3: Both mentors and mentees benefit from mentorship, gaining opportunities for learning and growth.

Exercise 5- Text 4:
1. Feedback entails comments and suggestions about job performance.
2. Employees can receive positive and constructive feedback.
3. Receiving feedback helps employees improve their work and grow professionally.
4. Constructive feedback helps employees identify areas for improvement.
5. Both employers and employees should seek feedback.

Exercise 6- Incidents Related to Job Performance and Training:
1. Jane was praised for her teamwork skills.
2. Jane needed to improve her time management.
3. Mark felt overwhelmed by the new software.
4. Mark's mentor offered additional guidance to help him.
5. Maria learned about the company's safety protocols and equipment usage.

Exercise 7- Strategies for Getting a Promotion:
1. Setting goals helps set a clear path for career advancement.
2. Taking on additional responsibilities shows initiative and capability.
3. Employees should use the feedback to improve their performance.
4. Continuous learning keeps your skills relevant, which makes you competitive.
5. Building strong relationships helps in networking and collaboration.

Exercise 8- Fill-in-the-Blanks:
1. Training
2. Evaluation
3. Mentor
4. PPE
5. Feedback
6. Promotion

Lesson 4: Effective Communication in the Workplace

Objectives for the Lesson:

- Students will learn vocabulary related to effective workplace communication.

- Students will read and answer questions on the various forms of communication in the workplace.

Exercise 1- Draw a line connecting each word to its correct definition.

Word	Meaning
Email	A person who oversees workers
Colleague	The skill, good judgment, and polite behavior expected at work
Feedback	A serious disagreement or argument
Customer	The exchange of information
Supervisor	A message sent electronically
Conflict	Information about someone's performance
Communication	A person who buys goods or services
Professionalism	A person you work with

Exercise 2- Read the text below before answering the questions.

In-Person Communication

In-person communication is a common way of interacting in the workplace. It involves face-to-face conversations, which allow for immediate feedback and clarification. Non-verbal cues, such as body language and facial expressions, play a significant role in these interactions. They can help convey emotions and attitudes.

Clear and respectful communication is essential in face-to-face interactions. It is important to listen actively, make eye contact, and respond appropriately. Effective in-person communication can lead to better teamwork and understanding among colleagues. It is also crucial for building trust and rapport in professional relationships.

Comprehension Questions:

1. What is in-person communication?

____

2. Why are non-verbal cues important?

____

3. What are some non-verbal cues mentioned in the text?

____

4. How can effective in-person communication benefit teamwork?

____

5. Why is listening actively important?

____

6. Summarize each paragraph in your own words.

____

Exercise 3- Read the text below before answering the questions.

Communicating via Email

Email is a widely used form of communication in the workplace. It allows for quick and efficient exchange of information. Emails can be formal or informal, depending on the context and the recipient. However, it's essential to maintain professionalism in all email communications.

When writing emails, it is important to be clear and concise. The subject line should indicate the purpose of the email. The body should include all necessary details, and the message should be polite and respectful. Emails are a permanent record of communication, so it is crucial to proofread them before sending them.

Comprehension Questions:

1. What is the purpose of a subject line in an email?

____

2. Why is it important to be clear and concise in emails?

____

3. What should be included in the body of an email?

____

4. How should the tone of an email be maintained?

____

5. Why is proofreading emails important?

____

6. Summarize each paragraph in your own words.

____

Exercise 4- Read the text below before answering the questions.

Communicating with Supervisors and Colleagues

Effective communication with supervisors and colleagues is key to a productive work environment. It involves understanding the appropriate tone and level of formality. When communicating with supervisors, it is important to be respectful and direct. Clarity is crucial, as it helps prevent misunderstandings.

While communication with colleagues can be more informal, it should still be professional, clear and respectful. Open communication fosters collaboration and helps resolve conflicts. Being a good communicator also involves listening to others and considering their perspectives.

Comprehension Questions:

1. Why is clarity important when communicating with supervisors?

____

2. How should you communicate with colleagues?

____

3. What can open communication help achieve?

____

4. Why is it important to listen to others?

____

5. How can communication prevent misunderstandings?

____

6. Summarize each paragraph in your own words.

Three (3) Examples of Bad Communication at Work

1. Example 1: John sent a brief email without a subject line, leaving his colleagues confused about the email's purpose.

2. Example 2: Sarah interrupted her colleague during a meeting, which led to a misunderstanding about the project's timeline.

3. Example 3: Mark failed to provide feedback to his team, resulting in repeated mistakes and low morale.

Comprehension Questions:

1. What was missing from John's email?

---

2. How did Sarah's interruption affect the meeting?

---

3. What was the consequence of Mark not providing feedback?

---

4. Why is a subject line important in an email?

---

5. How can interruptions lead to misunderstandings?

Exercise 6- Read the checklist below before answering the questions.

---

8 Tips for Excellent Customer Service and Communication at Work

- o   Greet customers warmly.

- o   Listen to customer concerns attentively.

- o   Respond promptly and politely.

- o   Be patient and understanding.

- o   Maintain a positive attitude.

- o   Provide clear and accurate information.

- o   Follow up on customer requests.

- o   Apologize for any inconvenience and offer solutions.

Comprehension Questions:

1. Why is it important to greet customers warmly?

____

2. How should you listen to customer concerns?

____

3. What should you do after a customer makes a request?

____

4. Why is maintaining a positive attitude important?

____

5. What should you do if a customer faces an inconvenience?

____

Exercise 7- Fill in the blanks with the correct words (colleague, communication, feedback, email, supervisor, professionalism).

---

1. An ____________ is a message sent electronically.

2. A ____________ is someone you work with.

3. ____________ is the exchange of information.

4. ____________ is important in both verbal and non-verbal communication.

5. A ______________ can help resolve misunderstandings at work.

6. Providing ______________ helps improve work performance.

Exercise 8- Dictation

Your teacher will read some of the new words from Exercise 1. Write down what you hear.

____

____

Exercise 9- Writing

Write a paragraph to summarize what you know and learned about effective workplace communication.

____

____

____

____

____

____

____

ANSWER KEYS

Exercise 1- Vocabulary Matching:
1. Email - A message sent electronically
2. Colleague - A person you work with
3. Feedback - Information about someone's performance
4. Customer - A person who buys goods or services
5. Supervisor - A person who oversees workers
6. Conflict - A serious disagreement or argument
7. Communication - The exchange of information
8. Professionalism - The skill, good judgment, and polite behavior expected at work

Exercise 2- Text 1:
1. In-person communication is face-to-face interaction in the workplace.
2. Non-verbal cues help convey emotions and attitudes.
3. Some non-verbal cues are body language and facial expressions.
4. It can improve teamwork by fostering better understanding and collaboration among colleagues.
5. Listening actively ensures you understand and respond appropriately.
6. Paragraph 1: In-person communication involves face-to-face interactions, where non-verbal cues like body language are important for conveying feelings.
   Paragraph 2: Clear, respectful communication is key in face-to-face interactions, as it builds trust, improves teamwork, and strengthens professional relationships.

Exercise 3- Text 2:
1. The subject line indicates the purpose of the email.
2. Being clear and concise ensures the recipient can quickly understand the message.
3. The body should include all necessary details, presented clearly and respectfully.
4. The tone should be polite and respectful.
5. Proofreading is important because emails are permanent records of communication, and errors can impact professionalism and clarity.
6. Paragraph 1: An email is a common workplace communication tool that should always maintain professionalism.
   Paragraph 2: Emails should be clear, concise, and polite, with a relevant subject line and carefully proofread before sending.

Exercise 4- Text 3:
1. Clarity prevents misunderstandings.
2. Communication with colleagues should be professional, clear, and respectful.
3. Open communication can foster collaboration and conflict resolution.
4. Listening to others helps you understand their perspectives.
5. Being clear and direct can prevent misunderstandings.
6. Paragraph 1: Effective communication with supervisors should be respectful, clear, and direct to avoid misunderstandings.
   Paragraph 2: Communication with colleagues can be informal but must remain professional, as open communication encourages teamwork and conflict resolution.

Exercise 5- Three (3) Examples of Bad Communication at Work
1. The email was missing a subject line.
2. Sarah's interruption caused a misunderstanding about the project's timeline.
3. The lack of feedback led to repeated mistakes and low morale.
4. The subject line indicates the purpose of the email.
5. Interruptions can cause misunderstandings by disrupting the flow of communication, leading to incomplete or unclear information being shared.

Exercise 6- 8 Tips for Excellent Customer Service and Communication at Work
1. It sets a positive tone.
2. You should listen to customers' concerns attentively.
3. You should follow up on customer requests.
4. This makes the customer feel valued and gives them a positive experience.
5. Apologize and offer solutions.

Exercise 7- Fill-in-the-Blanks:
1. Email
2. Colleague
3. Communication
4. Professionalism
5. Supervisor
6. Feedback

REFLECTION ON LEARNING

Answer the following questions and discuss your responses with your teacher or classmates.

1. What reading strategies did you learn or practice in this unit?

2. What new concepts or words did you learn?

3. What reading challenges did you face?

4. What reading strategies do you need to improve?

5. What do you want your teacher to know?

Lesson 1: Taxes and Fees

Objectives for the Lesson:

- Students will learn and use vocabulary related to taxes and fees.

- Students will read and answer questions on the different types of taxes and fees in the US.

Exercise 1- Draw a line connecting each word to its correct definition.

Word	Meaning
Income tax	An amount subtracted from income before calculating taxes
Federal tax	An official inspection of an individual's or organization's accounts
Sales tax	A fraudulent scheme or operation
Transaction fee	Money returned to a taxpayer if too much tax was paid
Refund	A tax on the money people or businesses earn
Deduction	A charge for processing a payment
Audit	Taxes collected by the national government
Scam	A tax on the sale of goods and services

Exercise 2- Read the text below before answering the questions.

Understanding Income and Federal Taxes

In the United States, individuals and businesses are required to pay income taxes on their earnings. Income tax is a significant source of revenue for the federal government. The government uses this money to fund various public services, including education, healthcare, and infrastructure.

There are different types of income taxes, such as federal, state, and local taxes. Federal taxes are paid to the national government, while state and local taxes are paid to state and local governments.

People often receive refunds if they have paid more taxes than they owe. It's important to file taxes accurately to avoid audits and penalties.

Comprehension Questions:

1. What is the purpose of income taxes?

____

2. What is one service that is funded by the government?

____

3. Who pays federal taxes?

____

4. What happens if someone pays more taxes than they owe?

____

5. What can happen if taxes are not filed accurately?

____

6. What are the types of income taxes mentioned?

____

Exercise 3- Read the text below before answering the questions.

Sales Taxes in the United States

Sales tax is a tax on goods and services that is added at the time of purchase. The rate of sales tax varies from state to state and can even differ within states. Sales tax is collected by the retailer and then passed on to the state government.

Not all goods and services are subject to sales tax. For example, essential items like groceries and medicine may be exempt from sales tax in some areas. Understanding sales tax is important for both consumers and businesses, as it affects the total cost of goods and services.

Comprehension Questions:

1. What is sales tax?

____

2. How is sales tax collected?

____

3. How does the rate of sales tax vary?

____

4. Are all goods and services subject to sales tax?

____

5. What items may be exempt from sales tax, if any?

____

6. Who benefits from the collection of sales tax?

____

7. Summarize the passage in your own words.

____

Business and Transaction Fees

Businesses often charge transaction fees for processing payments. These fees can vary depending on the method of payment, such as credit cards or electronic transfers. They can also affect the overall pricing of goods and services. Transaction fees help businesses cover the costs associated with handling transactions.

In addition to transaction fees, businesses may also charge other fees, such as service fees or convenience fees. It's important for consumers to be aware of these fees when making purchases. Understanding these fees can help them make informed financial decisions.

Comprehension Questions:

1. What are transaction fees?

____

2. Why do businesses charge transaction fees?

____

3. How can transaction fees vary?

____

4. What can transaction fees affect?

____

5. What other types of fees might businesses charge?

____

6. Why is it important for consumers to understand transaction fees?

____

7. Summarize the passage in your own words.

____

Exercise 5- Read the tips below before answering the questions.

Tips to Avoid Federal Tax Scams
1. Use secure websites when filing taxes online.
2. Be wary of phone calls demanding immediate payment.
3. Do not share personal information over the phone.
4. Verify the identity of anyone claiming to be from the IRS.
5. Do not respond to suspicious emails asking for tax information.
6. Report any suspected tax fraud to the authorities.
7. Keep your tax documents safe and secure.
8. Use trusted tax professionals for help.
9. Understand that the IRS does not accept payment in gift cards.

Comprehension Questions:

1. Why is it important to use secure websites when filing taxes online?

____

2. What should you do if you receive a suspicious phone call about taxes?

____

3. How can you verify the identity of someone claiming to be from the IRS?

____

4. What should you do with your tax documents?

____

5. Why should you not respond to emails asking for tax information?

____

6. What questions about tax scams do you have?

____

Exercise 6- Read the receipts below before answering the questions.

Receipts with Sales Taxes and Transaction Fees

Receipt 1: FashionX Clothing Store

Item	Price	Sales Tax	Total
Shirt	$20.00	$1.20	$21.20
Pants	$40.00	$2.40	$42.40
Shoes	$60.00	$3.60	$63.60
Total	$120.00	$7.20	$127.20

Receipt 2: Transit Airline

Service	Price	Transaction Fee	Total
Ticket	$200.00	$5.00	$205.00
Baggage Fee	$30.00	$2.00	$32.00
Total	$230.00	$7.00	$237.00

Comprehension Questions:

1. What was the total sales tax for the items purchased at FashionX?

____

2. How much was the transaction fee for the airline ticket?

____

3. What was the total cost of the pants and shoes including sales tax?

____

4. What additional fee did Transit Airline charge besides the ticket price?

____

5. Why is it important to understand these fees on receipts?

____

6. How does sales tax affect the total price of purchased items?

____

Exercise 7- Fill in the blanks with the correct words (*scam, audit, sales tax, income tax, refund, transaction*).

1. An __________ is a tax on the money people and businesses earn.

2. __________ is a tax on goods and services.

3. A __________ fee is a charge for processing a payment.

4. People may receive a __________ if they overpay taxes.

5. An __________ is an official inspection of accounts.

6. A __________ is a fraudulent scheme or operation.

Exercise 8- Dictation

Your teacher will read some of the new words from Exercise 1. Write down what you hear.

____

____

Exercise 9- Writing

Write a paragraph to summarize what you know and learned about taxes and fees in the US.

____

____

____

____

____

ANSWER KEYS

Exercise 1- Vocabulary Matching:
1. Income tax - A tax on the money people or businesses earn
2. Federal tax - Taxes collected by the national government
3. Sales tax - A tax on the sale of goods and services
4. Transaction fee - A charge for processing a payment
5. Refund - Money returned to a taxpayer if too much tax was paid
6. Deduction - An amount subtracted from income before calculating taxes
7. Audit - An official inspection of an individual's or organization's accounts
8. Scam - A fraudulent scheme or operation

Exercise 2- Text 1:
1. The purpose is to fund public services.
2. Education is one of the public services.
3. Individuals and businesses pay federal taxes.
4. They receive a refund.
5. It can lead to audits and penalties.
6. Federal, state, and local taxes are mentioned.

Exercise 3- Text 2:
1. A sales tax is a tax on goods and services added at the time of purchase.
2. The tax is collected by the retailer, and then passed to the state government.
3. The rate varies from state to state and within states.
4. No, some items may be exempt.
5. Essential items like groceries and medicine may be exempt from sales taxes.
6. The state government benefits from sales tax collection.
7. Sales tax is a tax added to the price of goods and services at the time of purchase, collected by retailers and sent to the state government. The rate of sales tax differs. Some items might be exempt from sales tax. Understanding this tax is important.

Exercise 4- Text 3:
1. Transaction fees are charges for processing payments.
2. Businesses charge them to cover the costs associated with transactions.
3. They can vary depending on the payment method.
4. Transaction fees can affect the overall pricing of goods and services.
5. Businesses might also charge service fees or convenience fees.
6. It is important to understand so they can make informed financial decisions.
7. Businesses charge fees for processing payments, which can vary by payment method and affect overall prices. These fees cover transaction costs. Additionally, businesses may add service or convenience fees. Consumers need to be aware of these fees to make smart financial choices.

Exercise 5- Tips to Avoid Federal Tax Scams
1. Secure websites protect personal and financial information from fraud.
2. Do not provide personal information and report the call.
3. Ask for official identification and verify through the IRS.
4. You should keep them secure to prevent identity theft.
5. They may be scams attempting to steal your information.

Exercise 6- Receipts with Sales Taxes and Transaction Fees
1. The total sales tax was $7.20.
2. The transaction fee was $5.00.
3. The total cost was $106.00.
4. They charged a baggage fee of $30.
5. It is important to be aware of the total cost and to avoid unexpected charges.
6. Sales tax increases the final amount paid.

Exercise 7- Fill-in-the-Blanks:
1. Income tax
2. Sales tax
3. Transaction
4. Refund
5. Audit
6. Scam

Lesson 2: Civic Activities and Responsibilities

Objectives for the Lesson:

- Students will learn and use vocabulary related to civic responsibilities and activities.

- Students will read and answer questions on how to participate in civic duties and the benefits of civic engagement.

Exercise 1- Draw a line connecting each word to its correct definition.

Word	Meaning
Voting	The status of being a member of a country
Jury duty	A formal request for change
Community service	The act of making a choice in an election
Petition	Serving on a jury in a court
Tax	Legal entitlements of individuals
Citizenship	The duty to contribute to the community and society
Rights	Money paid to the government
Civic responsibility	Volunteering to help others in the community

Exercise 2- Read the text below before answering the questions.

Understanding Civic Responsibilities in the US

Civic responsibilities in the United States include duties like voting, paying taxes, and serving on a jury. These responsibilities are essential for maintaining a functional and fair society. Voting allows citizens to have a say in their government and its decisions.

Paying taxes is another key responsibility, as it helps fund public services like schools, roads, and emergency services. Jury duty is a civic obligation that helps ensure a fair trial system. When citizens serve on juries, they contribute to the justice system by deciding the outcomes of legal cases.

Comprehension Questions:

1. What are some civic responsibilities mentioned in the text?

____

2. Why is voting important in a democracy?

____

3. How do taxes benefit society?

____

4. What is the purpose of serving on a jury?

____

5. How does jury duty contribute to the justice system?

____

6. What are the consequences of not fulfilling civic responsibilities?

____

7. Summarize the passage in your own words.

____

Exercise 3- Read the text below before answering the questions.

Being a Good Citizen and Resident

Being a good citizen and resident involves more than just following the law. It includes being informed about public issues, respecting the rights of others, and participating in community activities. Good citizens also take responsibility for their actions and contribute to the common good.

Community involvement can take many forms, such as volunteering, participating in local government, or joining community groups. By staying informed and engaged, citizens help shape the society they live in. They also help protect the rights and freedoms that everyone enjoys.

Comprehension Questions:

1. What does it mean to be a good citizen?

____

2. How can citizens participate in their communities?

____

3. Why is staying informed about public issues important?

____

4. What are some ways to contribute to the common good?

____

5. How does community involvement benefit society?

____

6. Why is it important to respect the rights of others?

____

7. Summarize the passage in your own words.

____

Exercise 4- Read the text below before answering the questions.

Civic Activities and Participation in States and Cities

Civic activities and participation in local, state, and city governments are vital for a healthy democracy. Citizens can engage in these activities by attending town hall meetings, voting in local elections, and participating in public hearings. These actions allow citizens to voice their opinions and influence local policies.

Another way to participate is by signing petitions or joining advocacy groups. These activities can bring attention to important issues and promote change. Local governments often rely on citizen input to make decisions that benefit the community. Therefore, civic engagement is crucial for responsive and representative governance.

Comprehension Questions:

1. What are some ways to participate in local government?

____

2. Why is attending town hall meetings important?

____

3. How can signing petitions contribute to civic engagement?

____

4. What role do advocacy groups play in society?

____

5. Why is citizen input important for local government decisions?

____

6. How can civic activities influence public policy?

____

7. Summarize the passage in your own words.

____

Exercise 5- Read the poster below before answering the questions.

Benefits of Becoming a US Citizen
1. Right to vote in federal elections
2. Ability to apply for federal jobs
3. Access to federal benefits and assistance
4. Easier travel and re-entry into the US
5. Protection from deportation
6. Ability to sponsor family members for immigration
7. Full protection under US law

Comprehension Questions:

1. What is one benefit of becoming a US citizen?

____

2. How does citizenship provide job opportunities?

____

3. What are the travel benefits of US citizenship?

____

4. How can citizenship help in family immigration?

____

5. What protection does US citizenship offer against deportation?

____

6. Why is the right to vote important for citizens?

____

Exercise 6- Fill in the blanks with the correct words (*petition, tax, community, voting, jury, citizenship*).

1. ___________ is the act of making a choice in an election.

2. ___________ duty involves serving in a court to help decide legal cases.

3. ___________ service involves volunteering to help others in the community.

4. A ___________ is a formal request for change, often signed by many people.

5. ___________ is the money paid to the government to fund public services.

6. ___________ is the status of being a member of a country with rights and responsibilities.

Exercise 7- Dictation

Your teacher will read some of the new words from Exercise 1. Write down what you hear.

____

____

Exercise 8- Writing

Write a paragraph to summarize what you know and learned about civic activities and responsibilities.

____

____

____

____

____

____

____

ANSWER KEYS

Exercise 1- Vocabulary Matching:
1. Voting - The act of making a choice in an election
2. Jury duty - Serving on a jury in a court
3. Community service - Volunteering to help others in the community
4. Petition - A formal request for change
5. Tax - Money paid to the government
6. Citizenship - The status of being a member of a country
7. Rights - Legal entitlements of individuals
8. Civic responsibility - The duty to contribute to the community and society

Exercise 2- Text 1:
1. Voting, paying taxes, and serving on a jury are civic responsibilities.
2. It allows citizens to have a say in their government and its decisions.
3. Taxes fund public services like schools and roads.
4. Jury duty helps ensure a fair trial system.
5. By deciding the outcomes of legal cases.
6. By not fulfilling civic responsibilities, society may be less functional and fair.
7. Civic responsibilities in the US include voting, paying taxes, and serving on a jury. These duties help ensure a functional society by allowing citizens to influence government, support public services, and contribute to a fair legal system.

Exercise 3- Text 2:
1. It means being informed, respecting others and participating in the community.
2. Citizens can volunteer, participate in local government, and join community groups.
3. It helps citizens make informed decisions and contribute to society.
4. Volunteering, participating in local government, and joining community groups are some ways of contributing.
5. It builds a stronger community and protects everyone's rights.

6. It ensures everyone can enjoy their freedoms.
7. Being a good citizen means more than following the law; it involves being informed, respecting others, participating in community activities, and contributing to the common good.

Exercise 4- Text 3:
1. Attending town hall meetings, voting and participating in public hearings are ways to participate.
2. It provides a platform to voice opinions and concerns.
3. It can bring attention to issues and promote change.
4. They raise awareness and advocate for important issues.
5. It ensures that decisions benefit the community.
6. They can influence and shape public policy.
7. Civic participation in local government is essential for a healthy democracy, as it allows citizens to influence policies and decisions.

Exercise 5- Benefits of Becoming a US Citizen:
1. One benefit is the right to vote in federal elections.
2. It allows applications for federal jobs.
3. Easier travel and re-entry into the US are the benefits.
4. US citizens can sponsor family members for immigration.
5. US citizenship provides protection from deportation.
6. It allows citizens to influence the government and its decisions.

Exercise 6- Fill-in-the-Blanks:
1. Voting
2. Jury
3. Community
4. Petition
5. Tax
6. Citizenship

REFLECTION ON LEARNING

Answer the following questions and discuss your responses with your teacher or classmates.

1. What reading strategies did you learn or practice in this unit?

2. What new concepts or words did you learn?

3. What reading challenges did you face?

4. What reading strategies do you need to improve?

5. What do you want your teacher to know?

You have 70 minutes to answer 38 questions.

PART 1 - Read the texts before choosing the correct answer.

EARNINGS STATEMENT

COMPANY NAME
SOME CORPORATION 123
123 G. SILANG ST., KALAYAAN CITY 1234

Employee Name: Hope Marie Santos
SSN: xxx-xx-6789
Employee ID: 98856

Check No: 98765
Pay Period: 5/1/2025-5/15/2025
Pay Date: 5/21/2025

Income	Rate	Hours	Current Total	Deductions	Current Total	Year-To-Date
Gross Wages	15.00	40	600.00	FICA MED TAX	8.70	78.30
				FICA SS TAX	37.20	334.80
				FED TAX	90.00	810.00
				NC ST TAX	34.50	310.50
				HEALTH	₱76.58	₱689.22
				DENTAL	₱8.23	₱74.07
				RETIREMENT	₱60.00	₱540.00

YTD GROSS	YTD DEDUCTIONS	YTD NET PAY	CURRENT TOTAL	CURRENT DEDUCTIONS	NET PAY
5,400	2,836.89	2,563.11	600.00	315.21	284.79

*Excluded from federal taxable wage

1. What does the 'Gross Wages' section represent on a paystub?

    a) The total amount earned before deductions

    b) The total amount after deductions

    c) The amount earned from bonuses

    d) The total tax amount deducted

2. If the 'Net Pay' is $284.79, what does it indicate?

    a) The total amount before taxes

    b) The amount paid after taxes and deductions

    c) The total deductions made

    d) The amount paid in taxes

MEMO

TO: All Employees

FROM: Human Resources Department

DATE: 8 March 2024

SUBJECT: Policy Reminder - Dress Code

MESSAGE:

Dear Team,

This memo serves as a reminder of our company's dress code policy. As stated in the employee handbook, business attire is required Monday through Thursday, and casual attire is permitted on Fridays.

If you have any questions regarding the dress code policy, feel free to reach out to the HR department. Thank you for your attention to this matter.

Regards,
Human Resources Department

DT STELLAR INDUSTRIES

(795) 948-9640 | hr@stellar.com
48 Hollis St, Westside, MA

3. On what day of the week is casual attire permitted according to the dress code memo?

   a) Monday

   b) Wednesday

   c) Thursday

   d) Friday

4. If an employee has questions about the dress code policy, who should they contact?

   a) The CEO

   b) The HR department

   c) Their manager

   d) The finance department

RESIDENTIAL LEASE AGREEMENT

1. **PARTIES.** This Residential Lease Agreement ("Agreement") made on **MONDAY 15TH APRIL, 2024** is between:

    Landlord Name: **ERIC SMITH** with a mailing address of:
    7427 MAPLE STREET, INDIANAPOLIS, IN 46201 ("Landlord"), AND

    Tenant Name(s): **LUISA CARTER** with a mailing address the same as the rental property ("Tenant").

2. **PROPERTY.** The Landlord agrees to lease the described property to the Tenant:

    Mailing Address: 5634 OAK AVENUE, INDIANAPOLIS, IN 46204

    Residence Type: ☐ Single-family ☒ Apartment ☐ Condo ☐ Other:

3. **TERM.** The Agreement shall begin on **MAY 1st, 2024** and end on **APRIL 30TH, 2024**.

4. **RENT.** The Tenant shall pay the Landlord in equal monthly installments of **$1200**. The Rent is due on the **1st** of every month and must be paid by: **DIRECT DEPOSIT**.

5. **SIGNATURES.**

    Landlord Signature: _______________________

    Printed Name: **ERIC SMITH**

    Tenant Signature: _______________________

    Printed Name: **LUISA CARTER**

5. According to the lease agreement, what is the monthly rent amount?

    a) $1200

    b) $1500

    c) $1800

    d) $2000

6. What is the type of residence mentioned in the lease agreement?

    a) Single-family

    b) Apartment

    c) Condo

    d) Townhouse

ANX PUBLISHING   16 June 2025

BILLED TO:

Arivaci & Co.
Phone No.: +123-456-7890
63 Ivy Road, Hawkville, GA, USA

PAYABLE TO:

Briard Bank
Account Name: Legend Books
Account No.: 123-456-7890

ITEM	HOURS	UNIT PRICE	TOTAL
Reach (Novel)	1	$123	$123
Jacket Back (Graphic Novel)	2	$127	$254
Penned and Left (Biography)	1	$123	$123
		Subtotal:	$500
		Tax (0%):	$0
Thank you!		**Total:**	**$500**

123 Anywhere St.,
Any City, ST 12345

(123) 456-7890
hello@reallygreatsite.com

7. What is the total amount billed on the invoice?

    a) $254

    b) $500

    c) $123

    d) $127

8. What is the service provided by the invoice for 'Jacket Back (Graphic Novel)'?

    a) 1 hour at $123

    b) 2 hours at $127

    c) 1 hour at $127

    d) 2 hours at $123

JOB VACANCY

We are a growing company seeking a motivated individual to join our team.

The position we have available is:

- Software Engineer
- Graphic Designer
- Sales Associates
- Software Development

APPLY NOW

 123-456-7890    www.reallygreatsite.com    123 Anywhere St., Any City

9. Which position is not listed in the job posting?

   a) Software Engineer

   b) Graphic Designer

   c) Sales Associates

   d) Marketing Manager

10. What action is suggested at the end of the job posting?

   a) Apply now.

   b) Contact HR.

   c) Visit the office.

   d) Send an email.

PART 2- Read the texts before choosing the correct answer.

Finding a Job in the US

Finding a job in the US involves several steps. First, it is important to have a well-prepared resume. A resume should include your work experience, education, and skills. Many people use online job search websites like Indeed or LinkedIn to find job listings. Networking is also a key part of finding a job. This means talking to people you know and attending job fairs to meet potential employers.

Once you find a job you are interested in, the next step is the application process. This often involves submitting your resume and a cover letter. A cover letter is a brief introduction that explains why you are interested in the job and why you would be a good fit. If the employer is interested in your application, they may invite you for an interview. The interview is an important part of the job search process. It is your chance to show the employer that you are the right person for the job. It is important to dress professionally and to be prepared to answer questions about your experience and skills.

Questions:

11. What is the first step in finding a job in the US?

    a) Submitting a cover letter

    b) Preparing a resume

    c) Attending job fairs

    d) Networking

12. What is the purpose of a cover letter?

    a) To list your work experience

    b) To provide references

    c) To describe your education

    d) To introduce yourself and explain your interest in the job

13. What should you do if an employer invites you for an interview?

    a) Send another resume.

    b) Dress professionally and prepare to answer questions.

    c) Ask for a higher salary.

    d) Decline the interview.

14. Which online job search websites are mentioned in the text?

    a) Indeed and Glassdoor

    b) LinkedIn and Monster

    c) Indeed and LinkedIn

    d) Monster and Glassdoor

In the US, individuals and businesses are required to pay various taxes. The two main types of taxes are federal and state taxes. Federal taxes are collected by the Internal Revenue Service (IRS) and are used to fund national programs such as defense, social security, and infrastructure. State taxes are collected by the state governments and are used for state-specific programs like education and transportation.

Besides taxes, businesses often have to pay different types of fees. These can include business license fees, registration fees, and transaction fees. Business license fees are required to legally operate a business in a specific location. Registration fees are paid when a business registers with the state. Transaction fees are charges that businesses must pay for certain types of financial transactions, such as credit card processing fees.

Paying taxes and fees is a legal requirement and failing to do so can result in penalties. It is important for both individuals and businesses to understand their tax obligations and to pay their taxes on time. Many businesses hire accountants or tax professionals to help them manage their taxes and fees effectively.

Questions:

15. What are the two main types of taxes in the US?

    a) Sales and property taxes

    b) Federal and state taxes

    c) Income and business taxes

    d) Local and regional taxes

16. What is the purpose of federal taxes?

    a) To fund state-specific programs

    b) To fund national programs like defense and social security

    c) To pay for local infrastructure

    d) To support small businesses

17. What are business license fees used for?

    a) To process credit card transactions

    b) To register a business with the state

    c) To legally operate a business in a specific location

    d) To pay federal taxes

18. What can happen if individuals or businesses fail to pay their taxes and fees?

    a) They can face penalties

    b) They will receive a reward

    c) They will be exempt from future taxes

    d) They can pay the taxes later without consequences

In the US, being an active citizen involves participating in civic responsibilities and activities. Civic responsibilities include actions like voting in elections, serving on a jury, and obeying laws. Voting is one of the most important civic responsibilities. It allows citizens to have a say in who represents them in government and in decisions that affect their community.

Besides voting, there are many ways to participate in civic activities. This can include attending town hall meetings, volunteering in the community, and joining local organizations. Civic activities help strengthen the community and ensure that everyone's voice is heard. Participating in these activities can also help individuals stay informed about local issues and contribute to making positive changes.

Becoming a US citizen comes with additional responsibilities and privileges. Naturalized citizens, those who were not born in the US but have become citizens, have the same rights and responsibilities as native-born citizens. This includes the right to vote and the duty to serve on a jury if called upon. Active participation in civic duties is essential for a healthy democracy and a strong community.

Questions:

19. What is one of the most important civic responsibilities mentioned in the text?

    a) Obeying laws

    b) Serving in the military

    c) Attending town hall meetings

    d) Voting in elections

20. What is one benefit of participating in civic activities?

    a) Receiving financial rewards

    b) Ensuring that everyone's voice is heard

    c) Avoiding taxes

    d) Getting a government job

21. Who has the same rights and responsibilities as native-born US citizens?

    a) Naturalized citizens

    b) Permanent residents

    c) Visitors

    d) Temporary workers

22. What is essential for a healthy democracy and a strong community?

    a) Active participation in civic duties

    b) Avoiding civic activities

    c) Following only federal laws

    d) Paying taxes on time

Workplace Safety Standards

Workplace safety is a critical aspect of any job. Companies must follow safety standards and procedures to ensure the well-being of their employees. These standards are often set by government agencies like the Occupational Safety and Health Administration (OSHA). OSHA provides guidelines on various safety practices, including the use of protective equipment, emergency procedures, and hazard communication.

Employees must be trained on these safety standards and procedures. This training includes understanding how to use safety equipment, knowing the location of emergency exits, and following proper lifting techniques to avoid injuries. Regular safety drills and meetings are conducted to keep everyone informed and prepared for potential emergencies.

Employers are responsible for maintaining a safe work environment. This includes conducting regular inspections, providing necessary safety gear, and addressing any safety concerns raised by employees. Employees, on the other hand, must adhere to safety protocols and report any unsafe conditions. A collaborative effort between employers and employees is essential to ensure a safe and healthy workplace.

Questions:

23. Who sets the guidelines for workplace safety standards?

    a) Employers

    b) Employees

    c) OSHA

    d) Local governments

24. What is one of the responsibilities of employees regarding workplace safety?

    a) Ignoring safety protocols

    b) Reporting unsafe conditions

    c) Avoiding safety training

    d) Conducting inspections

25. What should be included in employee training on safety standards?

    a) Proper lifting techniques

    b) Financial management

    c) Marketing strategies

    d) Customer service skills

26. What is a collaborative effort essential for?

    a) Increasing profits

    b) Ensuring a safe and healthy workplace

    c) Reducing taxes

    d) Improving customer satisfaction

Navigating Healthcare in the US

Accessing healthcare services in the US can be complex, but understanding the system can make it easier. The first step is to have health insurance. Health insurance helps cover the cost of medical services. There are different types of health insurance, including employer-provided insurance, government programs like Medicare and Medicaid, and private insurance plans.

Finding a primary care doctor is an important part of maintaining your health. A primary care doctor provides routine check-ups, treats illnesses, and can refer you to specialists if needed. To find a good doctor, you can ask for recommendations from friends or family, check online reviews, and ensure the doctor is covered by your insurance plan.

Healthcare services in the US include preventive care, emergency care, and specialist care. Preventive care involves regular check-ups and screenings to catch health issues early. Emergency care is for urgent medical situations, and specialist care is for specific health conditions that require expert attention. Understanding your health insurance coverage and knowing where to go for different types of care can help you navigate the healthcare system effectively.

Questions:

27. What is the first step to accessing healthcare services in the US?

a) Finding a specialist

c) Going to the emergency room

b) Having health insurance

d) Asking for recommendations

28. What type of care involves regular check-ups and screenings?

a) Preventive care

c) Specialist care

b) Emergency care

d) Dental care

29. What should you consider when finding a primary care doctor?

a) Their office location only

c) Their age and gender

b) Online reviews and insurance coverage

d) Their specialty only

30. What are government programs mentioned in the text that provide health insurance?

a) Medicare and Medicaid

c) Food Stamps and Social Services

b) Social Security and Unemployment Insurance

d) Public Housing and Child Care Assistance

Understanding K-12 Education

The US education system includes K-12 schools, which cover kindergarten through 12th grade. Public schools are funded by the government and are free for students to attend. Private schools, on the other hand, require tuition fees and may have different educational approaches or religious affiliations. Charter schools are another option, offering more flexibility in their curricula and often focusing on specific educational themes.

Elementary schools generally include kindergarten through 5th grade, middle schools cover 6th through 8th grade, and high schools encompass 9th through 12th grade. Each school level has its own set of standards and subjects that students must learn. For example, high school students take subjects like math, science, English, and history, along with elective courses such as art and physical education.

In addition to traditional subjects, many schools offer extracurricular activities like sports, music, and clubs. These activities provide students with opportunities to develop new skills and interests outside of the regular classroom. Participation in extracurricular activities is encouraged as it can enhance a student's overall educational experience and help with college applications.

Questions:

31. What are the three main levels of K-12 education in the US?

    a) Kindergarten, Elementary, and High School

    b) Middle School, High School, and College

    c) Elementary, Middle, and High School

    d) Preschool, Elementary, and Middle School

32. What type of schools requires tuition fees?

    a) Public schools

    b) Private schools

    c) Charter schools

    d) Community schools

33. What subjects are typically taught in high school?

    a) Math, Science, English, and History

    b) Art, Physical Education, and Cooking

    c) Philosophy, Sociology, and Anthropology

    d) Computer Science, Engineering, and Medicine

34. What are extracurricular activities, and why are they important?

    a) Regular classroom subjects; for extra credits

    b) Activities outside the classroom; for skill and interest development

    c) After-school jobs; for earning money

    d) Summer school programs; for additional learning

Managing household finances is essential for financial stability and peace of mind. The first step is to create a budget. A budget helps you track your income and expenses, ensuring that you do not spend more than you earn. To create a budget, list all your sources of income and all your monthly expenses, such as rent, utilities, groceries, and transportation.

Another important aspect of managing finances is saving money. It is advisable to save a portion of your income each month for emergencies and future expenses. This can include saving for a vacation, a new car, or unexpected medical bills. Setting up a separate savings account can help you keep your savings organized and avoid spending it on daily expenses.

Paying off debt is also a crucial part of financial management. High-interest debts, such as credit card balances, should be paid off as quickly as possible. This can save you money on interest payments and help improve your credit score. Additionally, it is important to plan for the future by investing in retirement accounts and other long-term savings plans. Managing your finances wisely can help you achieve your financial goals and provide security for your family.

Questions:

35. What is the first step in managing household finances?

    a) Investing in stocks

    b) Buying a new car

    c) Paying off credit card debt

    d) Creating a budget

36. Why is it important to save money?

    a) For emergencies and future expenses

    b) To buy luxury items

    c) To lend to friends

    d) To spend on daily expenses

37. What should you do with high-interest debts?

    a) Ignore them.

    b) Pay them off quickly.

    c) Transfer them to another credit card.

    d) Take out more loans.

38. How can you plan for the future financially?

    a) Spend all your money on current expenses.

    b) Avoid investing in retirement accounts.

    c) Invest in retirement accounts and long-term savings plans.

    d) Borrow money from friends and family.

PRACTICE TEST ANSWER KEYS

Part 1 - Visual Materials

Paystub

- o Question 1: Answer - a) The total amount earned before deductions
- o Question 2: Answer - b) The amount paid after taxes and deductions

Dress Code Memo

- o Question 3: Answer - d) Friday
- o Question 4: Answer - b) The HR department

Lease Agreement

- o Question 5: Answer - a) $1200
- o Question 6: Answer- b) Apartment

Invoice

- o Question 7: Answer - b) $500
- o Question 8: Answer - c) 1 hour at $127

Job Posting

- o Question 9: Answer - d) Marketing Manager
- o Question 10: Answer - a) Apply now.

Part 2 - Reading Texts

Finding a Job in the US

- Question 11: Answer - b) Preparing a resume
- Question 12: Answer - d) To introduce yourself and explain your interest in the job
- Question 13: Answer - b) Dress professionally and prepare to answer questions
- Question 14: Answer - c) Indeed and LinkedIn

Understanding Taxes and Fees in the US

- Question 15: Answer - b) Federal and state taxes
- Question 16: Answer - b) To fund national programs like defense and social security
- Question 17: Answer - c) To legally operate a business in a specific location
- Question 18: Answer - a) They can face penalties.

Being an Active Citizen

- Question 19: Answer - d) Voting in elections
- Question 20: Answer - b) Ensuring that everyone's voice is heard
- Question 21: Answer - a) Naturalized citizens
- Question 22: Answer - a) Active participation in civic duties

Workplace Safety Standards

- Question 23: Answer - c) OSHA
- Question 24: Answer - b) Reporting unsafe conditions
- Question 25: Answer - a) Proper lifting techniques
- Question 26: Answer - b) Ensuring a safe and healthy workplace

Navigating Healthcare in the US

- Question 27: Answer - b) Having health insurance
- Question 28: Answer - a) Preventive care
- Question 29: Answer - b) Online reviews and insurance coverage
- Question 30: Answer - a) Medicare and Medicaid

Understanding K-12 Education

- Question 31: Answer - c) Elementary, Middle, and High School
- Question 32: Answer - b) Private schools
- Question 33: Answer - a) Math, Science, English, and History
- Question 34: Answer - b) Activities outside the classroom; for skill and interest development

Managing Household Finances

- Question 35: Answer - d) Creating a budget
- Question 36: Answer - a) For emergencies and future expenses
- Question 37: Answer - b) Pay them off quickly
- Question 38: Answer - c) Invest in retirement accounts and long-term savings plans

REFLECTION ON LEARNING

Answer the following questions and discuss your responses with your teacher or classmates.

1. How do you feel about your performance on the practice test?

2. Was anything too hard for you? What was it?

3. Was anything too easy for you? What was it?

4. What reading strategies do you still need to review?

5. What else do you want your teacher to know?

ADULT ED
MATH
NUMBER SYSTEM, NUMBER SENSE, AND OPERATIONS PREPARING
FOR
CASAS, TABE 11 & 12, HISET, AND GED TESTING
BY COACHING FOR BETTER LEARNING

ADULT ED
MATH
GEOMETRY PREPARING
FOR
CASAS, TABE 11 & 12, HISET, AND GED TESTING
BY COACHING FOR BETTER LEARNING

CBL COACHING FOR BETTER LEARNING
Math
Practice Worksheets and Workbook for Adult Students
A learner-centered tool designed to help students practice and master the four operations while preparing them for CASAS Math GOALS 2, TABE 11 and 12, ACT, HISET, GED tests, and HiT programs.

SKILLS FOR SUCCESS IN CAREER AND TECHNICAL EDUCATION (CTE)
STUDENT GUIDE
A SYSTEMATIC WAY TO MASTER ORGANIZATIONAL AND SOFT SKILLS
CBL COACHING
BY COACHING FOR BETTER LEARNING, LLC.

HOW TO ACHIEVE BETTER STUDENT RETENTION IN ADULT EDUCATION
Secrets to becoming an indispensable adult-ed teacher that provides a learning experience that's hard to walk away from (and keeps administrators happy!)
TEDDY EDOUARD

TABE 11 & 12
CONSUMABLE STUDENT READING MANUAL
FOR LEVEL E
Preparing Adult Learners for TABE 11 & 12 Reading Tests and for Vocational Training and College Entrance Reading Exams
By Coaching for Better Learning, LLC

TABE 11 & 12
CONSUMABLE STUDENT READING MANUAL
FOR LEVEL M
Preparing Adult Learners for TABE 11 & 12 Reading Tests and for Vocational Training and College Entrance Reading Exams
By Coaching for Better Learning, LLC

TABE 11 & 12
CONSUMABLE STUDENT READING MANUAL
FOR LEVEL D
Preparing Adult Learners for TABE 11 & 12 Reading Tests and for Vocational Training and College Entrance Reading Exams
By Coaching for Better Learning, LLC

TABE 11 & 12
STUDENT LANGUAGE MANUAL
FOR LEVEL E
Preparing Adult Learners for TABE 11 & 12 Language Tests and for Vocational Training and College Entrance Exams
By Coaching for Better Learning, LLC

TABE 11 & 12
STUDENT LANGUAGE MANUAL
FOR LEVEL M
Preparing Adult Learners for TABE 11 & 12 Language Tests and for Vocational Training and College Entrance Exams
By Coaching for Better Learning, LLC

Preparing Adult Learners for TABE 11 & 12 Math Tests and for Vocational Training Entrance Math Exams
TABE 11 & 12
Consumable Student Math Workbook
FOR LEVEL E
By Coaching for Better Learning, LLC

Preparing Adult Learners for TABE 11 & 12 Math Tests and for Vocational Training Entrance Math Exams
TABE 11 & 12
Consumable Student Math Workbook
FOR LEVEL M
By Coaching for Better Learning, LLC

Preparing Adult Learners for TABE 11 & 12 Math Tests and for Vocational Training Entrance Math Exams
TABE 11 & 12
Consumable Student Math Workbook
FOR LEVEL D
By Coaching for Better Learning, LLC

Preparing Adult Learners for TABE 11 & 12 Math Tests and for Vocational Training Entrance Math Exams
TABE 11 & 12
Consumable Student Math Workbook
FOR LEVEL A
By Coaching for Better Learning, LLC

CBL COACHING FOR BETTER LEARNING
Workbook
Number and Letter Tracing for Adult Students
This tool is designed to help adult students practice and master handwriting. It is appropriate for literacy, ESL, and ABE classes.

READING NOTEBOOK & JOURNAL
For Adult Students
By Coaching For Better Learning   CBL COACHING

MATH NOTEBOOK & JOURNAL
For Adult Students
By Coaching For Better Learning   CBL COACHING

BOOK 1
PHONICS AND LIFE SKILLS READING FOR Adult Literacy, ABE, and ESL Students
Turning Learners into Proficient Readers
CBL COACHING FOR BETTER LEARNING

BOOK 2
PHONICS AND LIFE SKILLS READING FOR Adult Literacy, ABE, and ESL Students
Turning Learners into Proficient Readers
CBL COACHING FOR BETTER LEARNING

BOOK 3
PHONICS AND LIFE SKILLS READING FOR Adult Literacy, ABE, and ESL Students
Turning Learners into Proficient Readers
CBL COACHING FOR BETTER LEARNING

ABOUT CBL

At CBL, we promote systematic solutions, learner-centered textbooks, and forward-thinking strategies in adult education, workforce development, and vocational training. Our diverse solutions and products are intricately designed to enrich students' learning experiences while making the job of busy, hard-working adult instructors easier.

CBL takes pride in publishing student-centered textbooks designed to prepare learners for CASAS, TABE 11&12, HiSET, and GED assessments and to assist instructors in covering course curricula and standards with confidence.

Our publications also include teaching guides, test prep tools, and study guides that foster reflective learning, ensuring sustained engagement in active learning. Find our meticulously crafted textbooks on our book page (cbledu.com) or major platforms like Amazon, Barnes & Noble, and Ingram Spark.

CBL also guides adult education and workforce programs in establishing robust professional development programs—training, peer-mentoring, coaching, community of practices (CoPs), and instructional systems— fostering a culture of continuous improvement and contributing to higher learner retention and success rates. We also offer workshops and PD sessions for adult educators and classroom instructors.

If you have questions about instructional systems, textbooks, or student learning and retention, contact us today at teamcbl@cbledu.com or 410-960-4082.